MW00720876

Strategic Financial Decisions

The Financial Skills Series

The rapidly-changing role of the finance function in modern organisations is creating greater and more varied demands upon the skills of everyone involved in the world of finance and accounting. To enable busy professionals to keep up with this pace of change, Kogan Page has joined forces with the Chartered Institute of Management Accountants (CIMA) to create a lively, up-to-the-minute series of books on financial skills.

Highly practical in nature, each book is packed with expert advice and information on a specific financial skill, while the lively style adopted reflects the current dynamism of the discipline.

Already published in the series are:

Cost Control: A Strategic Guide
David Doyle
ISBN 0 7494 1167 8

Quality in the Finance Function
David Lynch
ISBN 0 7494 1145 7

Implementing an Accounting System
A Practical Guide
Revised Edition
Ray Franks
ISBN 0 7494 1052 3

Investment Appraisal
A guide for Managers
Revised Edition
Rob Dixon
ISBN 0 7494 1065 5

Strategic Financial Decisions
David Allen
ISBN 0 7494 1147 3

If you would like to be kept fully informed of new books in the series pleace contact the Marketing Department at Kogan Page, 120 Pentonville Road, London N1 9JN, *Tel* 071–278 0433, *Fax* 071–837 6348. CIMA members can also contact the Publishing Department at the Institute for further details of the series.

Strategic Financial Decisions

A Guide to the Evaluation and Monitoring of Business Strategy

DAVID
ALLEN

KOGAN
PAGE

First published in 1994

Apart from any fair dealing for the purposes of research or private study, or criticism or review, as permitted under the Copyright, Designs and Patents Act, 1988, this publication may only be reproduced, stored or transmitted, in any form or by any means, with the prior permission in writing of the publishers, or in the case of reprographic reproduction in accordance with the terms of licences issued by the Copyright Licensing Agency. Enquiries concerning reproduction outside those terms should be sent to the publishers at the undermentioned address:

Kogan Page Limited
120 Pentonville Road
London N1 9JN

© David Allen, 1994

British Library Cataloguing in Publication Data

A CIP record for this book is available from the British Library.

ISBN 0 7494 1147 3

Typeset by Photoprint, Torquay, S. Devon.
Printed and bound in Great Britain by Biddles Ltd, Guildford and Kings Lynn

Contents

Preface

The origins of this book go back to my experience in the Cadbury Schweppes group of companies. First as finance and logistics director of the beverages and foods division, and later as finance director of the confectionery division, I was conscious of major changes in the role of the finance function. Three aspects are worthy of mention in the present context:

☐ We were being asked to play a proactive role in making things happen, as well as reporting on what had happened.

☐ The difference between these two roles—decision support and monitoring respectively—was most marked at the strategic level of management, eg what businesses to be in, what products to offer, which markets to serve and so on.

☐ At this level, the traditional accounting model was not only inappropriate, but also potentially misleading: setting out to maximize this year's profit is almost certain to damage the long-term health of the business. Indeed, the widespread use of accounting numbers as a basis for measuring performance and rewarding managers is a significant contributor to the malaise of short-termism which plagues the English-speaking world.

At this time the accountancy profession was expending considerable effort on developing an approach to recognizing the impact of changing price levels. At Cadbury's we pioneered the 'comprehensive approach', which uplifted assets according to changes in their specific prices and made a capital maintenance provision according to the fall in the value of money. This never provided any useful information for management but it did draw attention to the real issue. It became clear that the limitations of the accounting model were not a fault of the particular definition of capital maintenance which was used; the problem lay in the concept of capital maintenance itself. Why focus only on tangible assets and the fall in the value of money—why not the value of the business and the cost of money?

From this question, and responding to the trends observed within that particular group, the concept of strategic financial management was born. It soon became apparent, however, that the trends affected enterprises across a wide range of industries in both the public and private sector. The concept was first made publicly available in a series of articles for *Accountancy Age*, and later as a thesis for a Master's degree at Loughborough University and a Report published by the *Financial Times*.

The essential features of the concept are:

☐ the recognition of two aspects of financial management —treasury and control;

☐ the linking of these by means of a principal financial objective of maximizing the net present value of the projected cash flows of the enterprise (discounted at the cost of capital), and a secondary objective (for private sector enterprises) of maximizing the proportion of that value which is attributable to the equity;

☐ the application of this objective to decision-making through a classification system which focuses on expected outcomes (as opposed to the backward-looking classification used in accounts) such as volume inducing, anticipative, sustaining, responsive or regenerative outlays;

☐ the use of the same logic for monitoring the outcome of decisions, through the mechanism of benchmarking.

The concept has received much attention in recent years. The president of the International Federation of Accountants has identified it as a major priority for that organization, the Chartered Institute of Management Accountants has introduced it as a subject in the final stage of its examinations and the *Financial Times* publication has gone to a third edition.

It is, however, regarded as revolutionary, in the sense that:

☐ many accountants are unable to come to terms with subjective judgements about an uncertain future (as opposed to objectively verifiable facts about a certain past) and choose to pass up the opportunity to be proactive financial managers;

☐ many managers protest that they are unable to think long term, given the sheer power of short-term financial controls such as profit budgets in the private sector or cash limits in the public sector.

This is compounded by the fact that most of the literature in this area is written by and for outsiders looking inwards and backwards. Cash flow, for example, is positioned as a function of profits, whereas the opposite is the case. The cost of capital is said to be a function of capital structure, whereas both are a function of perceived uncertainty. In particular, the cost of equity capital is said to be a function of past share prices, whereas the opposite is the case. Looking at these and other topics through the front windscreen rather than the rear-view mirror naturally produces a very different picture.

Those who do clear the hurdles of proactivity, long-termism and viewpoint, however, have a need for a more practical approach than is contained in any of the existing publications, and this book sets out to address that need.

After noting the links with the treasury function, the book focuses sharply on the control aspect of financial management in the context of an individual private sector business. It then looks at the limitations of accounting, focuses on financial management and offers a 'generic map' showing how the key control points—such as pricing and investments in various outlays—can be linked. In particular, it shows by means of a continuing example how relationship forecasts can be developed into decision-support information.

Among the ideas covered is that value is a forward-looking concept and may usefully be subdivided into faith, hope and expectations. The task of converting expectations into results receives a lot of attention—but who in your organization is responsible for raising hopes and converting them into expectations?

You will be prompted to think that while accounting can get

by with simple arithmetic, relationship forecasts require algebra and decision support can require the application of differential calculus. Whereas the balance sheet shows the sum of the costs not yet charged against revenue, the value of the business is the product of the interaction of its prevailing strategies.

You will also be prompted to think about management's dark continent: how do you ensure value for money in such areas as selling and distribution? Not by comparing actual with budget, or with last year, but by assessing the cost of the next best alternative. This has a natural affinity with the growing importance of the customer dimension of business —both in terms of formulating strategy and in monitoring progress.

In short, this is not a book which promises that, with slight modifications, your existing management accounting system can become suitable for the new industrial environment which is characterized by a rapid rate of change. It is a book which points out that the logic of accounting—though suitable for reporting on the past—is inappropriate to managing the future, and which offers you a financial management alternative.

The final chapter mentions other topics within the broad framework of the subject and invites readers to share in this exciting development. I look forward to hearing from you.

David Allen
Spring 1994

Strategic Financial Management

We are living through changing times, and the rate of change is increasing. In this chapter, we note some of the consequences of this situation, with particular reference to the need to be more strategic. At this level of management, the traditional accounting model is not just inappropriate, but dangerously misleading. A distinctive financial management model is offered, as a means of focusing on the value of an enterprise—for all practical purposes, in a commercial concern, the net present value of projected cash flows discounted at the cost of capital —and its use for decision support and progress monitoring is explored.

MANAGERIAL MEGATRENDS

When most of today's top managers were obtaining their basic managerial skills, the environment in which they operated was relatively stable. Administration skills were rated highly because, although some fine tuning might be required, there was an implicit assumption that tomorrow would be very much like yesterday. Today's environment, however, is best summed up by reference to its volatility and the best starting point is with the recognition that tomorrow is going to be different from yesterday. Simplicity and order have been replaced by complexity and chaos across the broad spectrum of society as we know it. Leadership skills are now seen to be paramount.

The causes of this volatility are varied and mutually

reinforcing. The accelerating pace of technological development and the liberalization of international trade are two fairly obvious factors. Indeed, the globalization of enterprise is a strong driving force as markets become more open and competitive. Different economies have different degrees of success in coping with this situation, resulting in ever more volatile rates of exchange, interest and inflation.

For the individual enterprise, this has prompted a shift in emphasis towards the strategic level of management (concerned with decisions as to what to do—the products to offer, the markets to serve, etc) as distinct from the tactical level (concerned with how to do what it has been decided should be done—the lead times to quote, the stocks to hold, etc). The more rapid the rate of change, the more frequently and the more quickly strategic issues have to be addressed.

Techniques such as budgetary control, based on the traditional accounting model, are very good at answering the question 'How well did we do what we chose to do?' but are not designed to answer questions like 'How well did we choose what to do?' or 'What should we do now?' As managers get to grips with these questions, they realize that the functionalism which provides excellence at the tactical level, and which budgetary control tends to reinforce, is an impediment at the strategic level. Here, they need a unifying generalism if they are to make the optimum trade-offs between such things as prices, volumes, quality and costs.

Old-fashioned, top-down command and control structures —setting objectives for others to achieve—are simply not sufficiently fast on their feet, close to customers or alert to competitive activities to be able to respond to change. Consequently, we are seeing a trend towards flatter and more devolved structures, in which empowerment is the order of the day. Privatization, unbundling and decentralization of wage bargaining are examples of this trend, but perhaps the clearest manifestation is the concept of 'strategic business units' within an enterprise.

In turn, this has highlighted the disadvantages of confrontation—between functions within an enterprise and between enterprises. In its place, we are seeing greater attention to teamwork within the business units, to strategic alliances and to partnership sourcing. At the macro level, the separation of ownership and control, typified by the quoted companies which are so prevalent in the English-speaking economies, is receiving increasing attention under the banner of 'corporate governance'.

At the same time, the tangible assets (such as property, plant and stock) which are so important in the context of the accounting model, and which are used as a basis for denominating directors' powers, are increasingly seen as strategic liabilities and poor indicators of the financial health of an enterprise. These days, sustainable competitive advantage is more likely to spring from the very investments which are classified as intangible—such as research, development, marketing, training and information—and therefore written off as they are incurred.

Likewise, quantity is giving way to quality, standardization to customization, and hard (inevitably backward-looking) measures of performance to soft (appropriately forward-looking) assessments of potential. It used to be said that if you couldn't measure it, you couldn't control it. Today, it is recognized that if you can measure it, so can the competition; the most powerful elements in any strategy are likely to be the ones which are extremely difficult, if not impossible, to measure—such as design, image, reputation and skill.

This is linked with another trend, away from a focus on the attributes of products towards a focus on the requirements of customers. Strategic reviews usually start with questions such as 'Who are our customers and what do they value?' In most cases, this calls for greater flexibility regarding the resources to be tapped, resulting in an increase in the proportion of costs which are shared across a range of products or customers, and which are insensitive to volume fluctuations.

Helping managers make decisions in these conditions has become less a matter of analysing data about a certain past and more a matter of synthesizing judgements about an uncertain future. The reductionist approach is out, the holistic approach is in. Management today is less about reacting to identified problems and more about proactively seeking opportunities. This is a particularly important trend as far as accountants are concerned because, traditionally, analysis has been their strong suit.

Indeed, it needs to be recognized that the limitations of the traditional accounting model render it quite inappropriate as a management tool, especially at the strategic level. Alongside it, there is a need for a financial management model—distinctive but, as will be seen later, capable of being reconciled to it. The nature of these limitations and the desirable features of a financial management model will be addressed later in this chapter.

If we summarize these trends—see Figure 1.1—we see two lists which are internally consistent. The left side is analogous to the *static* branch of a science, the right side to the *dynamic* branch. The left side rates age, experience and knowledge; the right side rates youth, enterprise and innovation. It is difficult to mix attributes from the two sides. The judgements required to arrive at an appropriate strategy, for example, are unlikely to be forthcoming in a confrontational organization, for fear of 'being taken down and used in evidence'.

The right side is more complex than the left and subject to what appear at first glance to be ambiguities. People—especially those based at the centre of organizations, eg group head offices—often ask:

☐ How can we be more strategic in conditions of volatility?

☐ How can we delegate authority without losing control?

☐ Does greater flexibility not mean less commitment?

☐ Does paying more attention to the long term not give the impression that the short term does not matter?

These apparent ambiguities can be reconciled but, in the process, the organization is likely to be transformed. The development of a structure of strategic financial management is a key part of such transformation.

ELEMENTS OF CONTROL

The more rapidly the environment is changing, the more outward looking the management of an enterprise needs to be. Specifically, it needs to enhance its:

☐ awareness of the environment in which it is operating;

☐ anticipation of changes in that environment;

☐ adaptability to those changes.

These may be thought of as the three As of strategic

FROM	TO
STABILITY	VOLATILITY
NATIONAL	GLOBAL
TACTICAL	STRATEGIC
FUNCTIONALISM	GENERALISM
CENTRALISED	DEVOLVED
CONFRONTATION	TEAMWORK
TANGIBLES	INTANGIBLES
QUANTITY	QUALITY
PRODUCTS	CUSTOMERS
DIRECT	INDIRECT
ANALYSIS	SYNTHESIS
REACTIVE	PROACTIVE
ACCOUNTING	FINANCIAL MANAGEMENT
STATIC	DYNAMIC

Figure 1.1 Managerial megatrends

management, of which the greatest is the third. There is no point in being acutely aware of environmental pressures and uncannily accurate in anticipating change if the organisation is not able to respond.

As portrayed in Figure 1.2, these essentials of strategic management prompt a recognition of the different kinds of information required to ensure control:

☐ Awareness suggests the need for monitoring information, which provides a record of what is happening. The accounting system contains a lot of monitoring information but needs to be augmented with more outward-looking data, such as market size and competitors' shares.

☐ Anticipation suggests forecasts, of which there are two subsets:

—relationship forecasts, eg what we think would happen to aggregate costs if volume were to be 10 per cent higher, or to aggregate volume if we lowered our selling prices by 5 per cent or doubled our investment in advertising;

—expected outcomes, eg the specific volume and cost consequences of decisions as to price and advertising.

☐ Adaptation puts a premium on decision-support information, eg identifying the optimum combination of prices and advertising against the criterion of a defined objective, such as the maximization of the net present value of projected cash flows.

These are interrelated in a way which is brought out in Figure 1.3. Accountability is achieved by comparing what is happening with what was expected to happen when a decision was made, and feeding this back into the learning process through which future decisions are improved. All too often, however, this logic is ignored. Even at the tactical level, it is often subordinated to a comparison of what is happening with what someone other than the decision-maker budgeted to happen. At the strategic level, more seriously, there is often a mismatch: investments may be approved on the basis of a discounted cash flow evaluation but if performance is measured and managers rewarded on the basis of accounting numbers, short-termism will be reinforced.

ESSENTIALS	INFORMATION
AWARENESS	MONITORING
ANTICIPATION	FORECASTS:
	RELATIONSHIP
	EXPECTED OUTCOME
ADAPTATION	DECISION SUPPORT

Figure 1.2 Strategic management

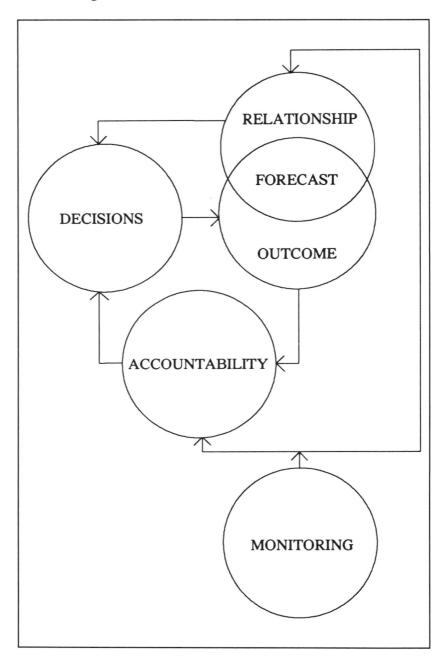

Figure 1.3 Elements of control

The problem is that performance measurement is, by definition, totally backward looking. It might be useful in short-cycle, repetitive situations which are frequently met at the operational level, and occasionally at the tactical level. Strategy, on the other hand, is essentially forward looking: decisions are based on an assessment of potential. The point is that you can't afford to wait until a strategy has been completed before measuring the outcome and hoping to learn the appropriate lessons. The monitoring of strategy needs to be continuous and forward looking. The spectacular collapses of recent years have shown how it is possible to report good performance while running down potential, not least by skimping on those 'intangible' investments.

To counteract this problem—which has contributed to the accountancy profession's expectation gap—it is necessary to recognize that there are no objectively verifiable facts about the future and to grasp the concept of the three Ps: progress equals performance plus or minus the change in potential. This is illustrated in Figure 1.4.

This brings us back to the question of why the traditional accounting model is unable to satisfy the needs of financial managers.

FINANCIAL MANAGEMENT DISTINGUISHED FROM ACCOUNTING

The origins of the accounting model are to be found in stewardship reporting: explaining to investors what has been done with their money. As time has gone by, accounts have also come to be used in a regulatory context—eg as inputs to taxation computations and to determine distributable profits. Such reports need to be endorsed by impartial outsiders who are not part of the action; words like regular, comparable —and therefore standardized—spring to mind. The financial manager, on the other hand, is an active insider, involved in the control of the enterprise and questions such as what to do with the money currently entrusted to the management. Here the operative words are likely to be sporadic, unique, and therefore customized.

Specifically, everything in accounting statements is, by

TIME FRAME	PAST	PRESENT	FUTURE
TASK	MEASURING	MONITORING	ASSESSING
FOCUS	PERFORMANCE	PROGRESS	POTENTIAL

RECONCILIATION:

PROGRESS = PERFORMANCE + / - CHANGE IN POTENTIAL

Figure 1.4   The fourth dimension

definition, backward looking. If figures are to be verified, the focus must be on what has already happened: as noted earlier, there are no facts about the future. This also explains why the accounting model makes no claim to assess the value created by an enterprise over time or its value at a point in time. It merely aims to assess how much of the wealth created has been realized in the form of tangible assets. Contrast this with the needs of those involved in decision-making, which is a totally forward-looking activity relying on judgements about an uncertain future. The focus is on wealth creation, implying the potential to realize it at a future date; until then, the assets are intangible.

Likewise, thanks to the need for objectivity, everything in accounting statements is inward looking, concentrating on costs and based on the concept of capital maintenance (profit for a period is defined as 'what an enterprise could afford to distribute and still be as well off as it was at the beginning of the period'). Decision-makers, on the other hand, need to be outward looking, concentrating on the perceived value of outcomes. Bear in mind, however, that value is subjective —like beauty, it is in the eye of the beholder—and cannot be accounted for until after the event.

Most significantly, however, it needs to be noted that capital maintenance is not a decision-making criterion. Financial management is not concerned with the question of *whether or not* capital is being maintained but *whether enough* wealth is being created to warrant the employment of the capital.

In short, the accounting model is, by design, a static one, concerned to allocate costs and revenues as between discrete, relatively short, time frames. To do this, it introduces concepts of revenue and capital, profits and assets. Financial management, on the other hand, is concerned with the dynamics of the business, not just this year but over the longer-term continuum. It has no need for those accounting concepts, being expressed in terms of cash flows, and is equally relevant in the public sector and in private but not-for-profit organizations.

The point of these contrasts is not to denigrate the accounting model, nor even to support the arguments being put forward to modify it in some way, eg to include intangibles or to carry assets forward at a value instead of cost. For, as it stands, the model is internally consistent: if you seek objective verifiability, you must focus on backward-looking costs. Rather, the point is to emphasize the need for an additional model which, by design, satisfies the needs of those charged with making the decisions which shape the future of the enterprise. Were they to use the accounting model for that purpose, they would undoubtedly sacrifice the long-term health of the enterprise on the altar of short-term reported profits or cash limits.

Figure 1.5 sums up these contrasts in a way which elaborates the relevant line on the 'megatrends' chart and reflects the two sides of the brain: the left which is used to analyse what exists, and the right, which is used to imagine what does not yet exist. It is not without significance that many accountants became so because they had particularly strong left sides to their brains. Making the transition to a task in which it is the right side which needs to dominate is not easy.

More seriously, there are numerous examples—especially in the English-speaking world—of enterprises which are obsessively oriented towards accounting and which have skimped on those investments which are not capitalized in order to maximize current earnings per share or to minimize current cash absorption. Overcoming this problem calls for a financial management model with its own distinctive features, and though, ideally, it should be capable of reconciliation with the accounting model which is so well known (if not really understood).

Strategic financial management is such a model.

CLARIFYING THE OBJECTIVE

The world of enterprise is characterized by a competitive struggle for existence—resources are finite, needs are infinite, and the economic question is about priorities. The discipline is most clearly seen in the private sector, where survival depends on being able to:

☐ identify genuine market needs, ahead of the competition;

☐ satisfy those needs better than the competition;

☐ offer the prospect of an adequate return on investment.

Thus the key to the working of the capitalist market economy is the prospective return on investment. Enterprises which can

ACCOUNTING	FINANCIAL MANAGEMENT
REPORTING	CONTROL
PASSIVE	PROACTIVE
IMPARTIAL	INVOLVED
STANDARDISED	CUSTOMISED
BACKWARD LOOKING	FORWARD LOOKING
VERIFIABLE	JUDGMENTAL
REALISED	POTENTIAL
TANGIBLE	INTANGIBLE
INWARD LOOKING	OUTWARD LOOKING
OBJECTIVE	SUBJECTIVE
COSTS	VALUES
CAPITAL MAINTENANCE	ADEQUATE RETURN
STATIC	DYNAMIC
DISCRETE	CONTINUUM
SHORT TERM	LONG TERM
PROFITS / ASSETS	CASH FLOW

Figure 1.5 Not only . . . but also

offer the prospect of an adequate return will be able to attract new funds and/or retain a proportion of internally generated funds, thereby enabling them to grow. Those falling short will not only find it impossible to attract new funds but will also be pushed into distributing some or all of their funds for more effective investment elsewhere. In this way, the strong points of the economy are fed and the weak points starved, leading to an overall improvement in its health. The evolution of enterprise is illustrated in Figure 1.6.

Financial management involves both heeding this discipline of the market-place and harnessing it as a basis for the allocation of resources as between the business units which constitute the entity. This suggests two aspects, external and internal.

The external aspect, normally referred to as the treasury function, is, in the context of financial decisions, concerned with the relationship between the entity and its financial stakeholders (shareholders, lenders and tax authorities). In a private sector context, and recalling the three As—awareness, anticipation and adaptation—the key tasks can be classified as:

☐ the *identification* of sources of financing, ranging from borrowings through various hybrids to equity capital;

☐ the *assessment* of the likely reward expectations of the providers, ie interest and dividends, not forgetting any associated taxes;

☐ the *employment* of the various sources to the extent, and in the proportions, deemed appropriate.

The internal aspect, normally referred to as the financial control function, is concerned with the relationship between the enterprise and its constituent business units. It has parallel tasks, notably:

☐ the *identification* of opportunities to invest in specific areas;

☐ the *assessment* of the likely returns on each;

☐ the *deployment* of funds in support of those opportunities considered to be worthwhile.

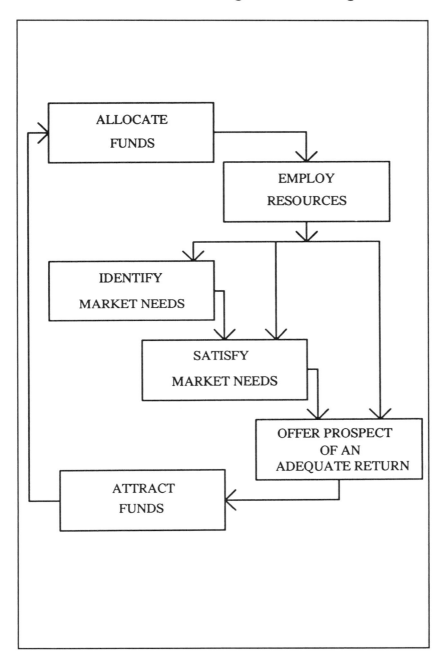

Figure 1.6   The evolution of enterprise

The links between the aspects are twofold, creating a control loop as shown in Figure 1.7. One link is what is variously referred to as the time value of money, the money value of time or the cost of capital. What the treasurer sees as the rate of return necessary to warrant the employment or retention of funds, the controller sees as the criterion for their deployment. The other link is the projection of cash flows. The controller is in a position to forecast the net cash generation or absorption of the enterprise; the treasurer interprets this in terms of the enterprise's ability to pay dividends or its need to raise more capital.

Putting these aspects together prompts the articulation of a unifying 'primary financial objective', namely:

> the maximization of the net present value of projected cash flows discounted at the cost of capital.

Unless capital can be invested to earn a return which covers the cost of capital, it should be returned to the financial stakeholders. The promulgation of such a clear objective is essential if the entity is to select, implement and monitor a coherent set of justifiable strategies. The twin foundations of financial management, therefore, are the cost of capital and cash flow.

As regards the first, the importance of the assessment of the cost of capital cannot be overstated. An entity which uses too high a figure will cede viable opportunities to its competitors, leading to stagnation or decline. One which uses too low a figure, on the other hand, will invest in uneconomic activities which will induce a liquidity crisis. One which gets it right will be in a position to reinforce areas of strength and abandon areas of weakness, thereby maximizing its chances of survival.

The discipline is less obvious in the public sector, in that disbelief can be suspended for long periods of time. In particular, the link between an adequate return on (tax-payers') funds and the attraction of those funds is subject to political manipulation, ie resources are allocated without any attempt to put a value on the expected outputs. However, given that the resources used are thereby denied to the private sector, there is a strong argument that the financial controls need to be at least as stringent.

From an economic point of view, the cost of capital is a

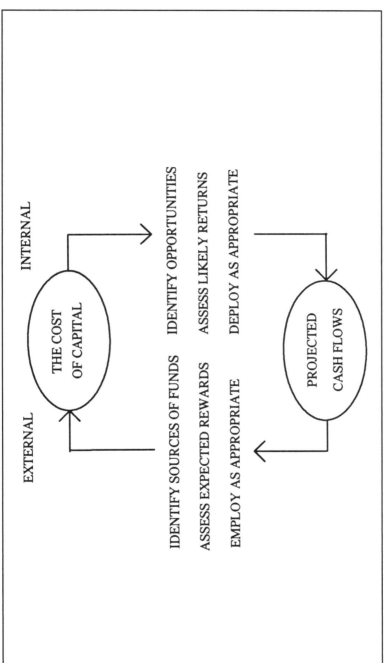

Figure 1.7 Two aspects of financial management

quantification of society's relative preference for cash flows in different time frames. As such, it is the same for all entities, irrespective of whether they are in the public or private sector (and, in the latter case, whether they are privately owned or publicly quoted) and it is independent of capital structure. Contrary to what academic theorists choose to presume, however, it is not a constant, nor is it the same for all time frames, and neither money markets nor taxation systems are neutral. In a private sector enterprise, therefore, there is a secondary (but vitally important) objective with which treasurers are especially concerned: the maximization of the proportion of the value of the entity which is attributable to the equity shareholders as distinct from lenders and the tax authorities. This is illustrated in Figure 1.8.

In most cases, this 'shareholder value' is the net present value of projected dividends, but it would be dangerous to presume that this equates with market capitalization, ie the number of shares in issue multiplied by the price which brought yesterday's supply and demand for small lots of the company's shares into equilibrium. This may cause conflicts in the minds of directors (especially if they have substantial share options) but logic says that they should focus their efforts on maximizing shareholder value as defined above and recognize the buying and selling of parcels of shares for the zero sum game that it is.

We now turn our attention to the second of the foundations of financial management: cash flow.

UNDERSTANDING CASH FLOW

For reasons associated with the requirements of taxation, company law and stock markets, the primary audience for published accounts is the general body of shareholders, ie the equity investors. The profit statement, for example, deducts from the operating profit of the enterprise the amounts appropriated to the other financial stakeholders in order to arrive at a figure of profit attributable to the equity. The balance sheet, likewise, deducts from the operating assets of the enterprise the amounts owing to the other financial stakeholders to arrive at a figure rarely labelled on the face of

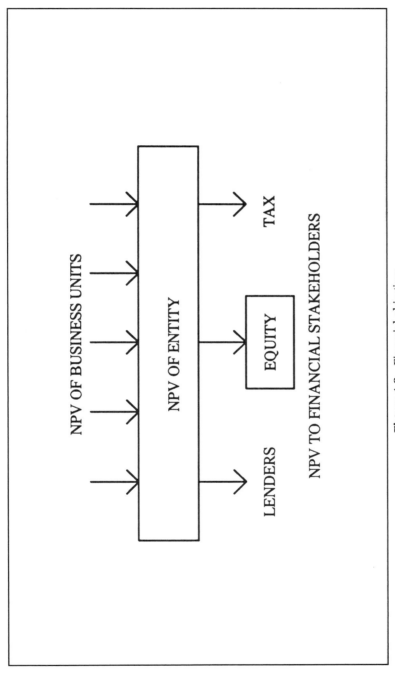

Figure 1.8 Financial objectives

the document but usually referred to as the net worth or net book value of the equity.

It is important to recognize that the equity investors represent only one particular group of outsiders looking in. There are other financial stakeholders, namely lenders and tax authorities, with their own, different, angles. Financial management operates within an entity and takes a correspondingly broader view, characterized again by external and internal aspects which are linked as follows:

☐ For any entity to function, it needs to attract *financing*, ranging from loans through hybrids to equity.

☐ Such financing provides the wherewithal for the entity to invest in *assets* to be employed in constituent business units.

☐ Managers employ these assets to satisfy market needs with a view to making *profits*.

☐ These profits are appropriated either as *distributions* (interest, tax and dividends) or as retentions.

☐ The retentions, effectively, augment external financing in terms of funding expansion. In other words, there are only two sources of funds for expansion: retentions or external financing.

This flow of funds is illustrated in Figure 1.9.

The relationship between an entity and its financial stakeholders can be expressed in terms of cash flow: if financing exceeds distributions, the entity is a net absorber of cash; if distributions exceed financing, it is a net generator of cash. Likewise, the relationship between an enterprise and its constituent businesses can also be expressed in terms of cash flow: businesses (and hence, in aggregate, enterprises) which are exhibiting expansion at a pace faster than can be financed by profits are net absorbers of cash; conversely, where profits exceed expansion, they are net generators of cash. Needless to say, these are two facets of the same cash flow:

Distributions		Profit
minus	equals	minus
Financing		Expansion

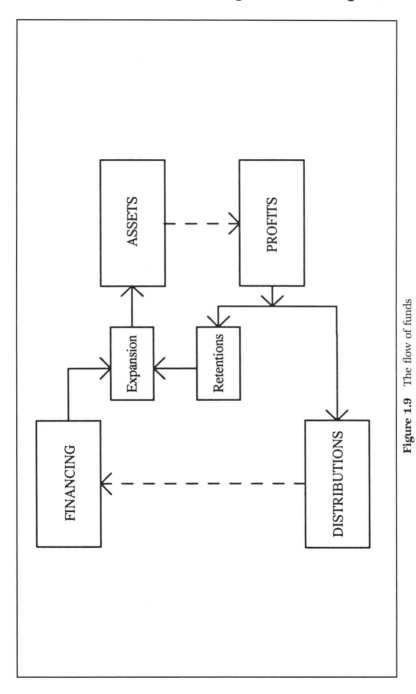

Figure 1.9 The flow of funds

The usual order of appearance in published accounts is (i) the profit statement, (ii) balance sheet and (iii) a cash flow statement which appears to have been derived therefrom, ie cash generation is seen as profit minus the expansion of assets. It is not without significance that this is a 'rear-mirror' view, ie precisely the opposite order to that in which the information becomes available. The net cash generation is known, unequivocally, almost immediately the period has ended but it takes weeks to apply the chosen accounting conventions, concepts and rules so as to identify those outlays which can be carried forward on the balance sheet. On the completion of that exercise, the profit figure appears. A 'front-windscreen' view of the process would correspond to the three Ps, as follows:

☐ Performance is measured as cash generation.

☐ Potential is assessed in terms of the unconsumed cost of the tangible assets.

☐ Progress is monitored in terms of profit, ie cash generation plus or minus the change in the unconsumed cost of the tangible assets.

As mentioned earlier in this chapter, the concept of capital maintenance is fundamental to the accounting model: 'profit is what you could afford to distribute and still be as well off as you were'. This begs the question, of course, as to how to measure well-offness. The traditional accounting model follows a historical–nominal convention, ie it calculates expansion as the difference between opening and closing tangible assets 'valued' at their historical costs, with no adjustment for any changes in either the specific prices of the assets or the general price level (the value of money).

LESSONS FROM THE 'ACCOUNTING FOR CHANGING PRICE LEVELS' EXPERIENCE

Applying different accounting conventions would produce different profit figures from the same unequivocal cash flow:

☐ Had we adopted a historical–real convention such as current (or general) purchasing power, we would have uplifted the asset figures and made a capital maintenance provision on the basis of the fall in the value of money.

☐ Had we adopted a current–nominal convention such as current cost accounting (CCA) we would have uplifted the asset figures and made a capital maintenance provision (confusingly disguised as cost of sales and monetary working capital adjustments) on the basis of the changes in their specific prices.

☐ Had we adopted a current–real convention such as the comprehensive approach, we would have uplifted the assets according to the changes in their specific prices and made a capital maintenance provision on the basis of the fall in the value of money (without any need for those complex 'adjustments' which characterized CCA).

This is not the place to go into the relative merits of the various conventions as far as financial reporting is concerned. It is the place, however, to note that none of the approaches commended themselves to managers proactively involved in the management of enterprises. The reason is not difficult to fathom: it is the capital maintenance point again. In practice, it is never a question of *whether or not* an accounting profit is being made—whether expressed in nominal, real or physical terms—but rather *whether enough* wealth is being created relative to the resources committed to the activity in question and the time frame of that commitment.

Nevertheless, the experience did help to highlight the limitations of the traditional accounting model and to identify what is required for financial management. Two adjustments are clearly required:

☐ We need to get away from the constraint associated with the focus on historical–nominal costs, but why recognize only those unrealized gains brought about by changes in the prices at which tangible assets are carried forward? What about those brought about, for example, by investments in intangibles? In fact, why not focus on what it is that management is seeking to maximize—the value of the business?

☐ We also need to recognize the passage of time, but why restrict this to inflation, which is only one element of the time value of money (the other being the real interest rate)? Why not focus on the criterion against which strategic decisions are made—the cost of capital?

By continuing to measure performance in the same way as the accounts (ie in terms of cash generation) but assessing potential differently (ie in terms of value rather than cost) it would be possible to monitor strategic progress in a way which could be reconciled to those accounts (the differences being unrealized gains and the cost of capital). We look at this in the next chapter.

2

A Control Framework

In this chapter, a worked example is introduced to clarify the concept of cash flow from an entity point of view, and to reconcile the output from the financial management model with that from the accounting model. The links between values at different points in time are explained and a framework is established which incorporates individual dimensions of strategy, and their blending into business and corporate strategies.

THE TRADITIONAL ACCOUNTING MODEL

In order to see how the principles touched on in the previous chapter work out in practice, let us set up a simple example of a company which has produced the results shown in Table 2.1.

In accordance with the requirements of FRS 3, the cash flow—for year 3, for example—would be summarized thus:

	£000	
Cash flow from operations		
Profit before depreciation	3,443	
(Increased net current assets)	(594)	
	2,849	
Returns on investment		
(Dividends paid)	(614)	
(Interest paid)	(341)	
		(955)
Taxation (paid)		(640)
Investment		
Capital expenditure		(1,474)
(Increased borrowings)		(220)

Significantly, this layout does not actually highlight the net cash generation/(absorption) of the enterprise. The cash flow equation, referred to in the previous chapter, does, as shown in Table 2.2.

Table 2.1 Balance sheets and profit statements

	Closing balance sheets		
	Year 1	Year 2	Year 3
	£000	£000	£000
Operating assets			
Fixed	4,600	5,060	5,566
Net current	5,400	5,940	6,534
	10,000	11,000	12,100
(Borrowings)	(2,000)	(2,200)	(2,420)
(Tax provision)	(582)	(640)	(704)
Equity	7,418	8,160	8,976
(Dividends payable)	(558)	(614)	(675)
Net worth	6,860	7,546	8,301
Issued capital	5,000	5,000	5,000
Reserves	1,860	2,546	3,301
Net worth	6,860	7,546	8,301
	Profit statements		
Profit before depreciation	2,846	3,130	3,443
(Depreciation)	(800)	(880)	(968)
Operating profit	2,046	2,250	2,475
(Interest payable)	(283)	(310)	(341)
(Taxes payable)	(582)	(640)	(704)
(Dividends payable)	(558)	(614)	(675)
Increase in reserves	623	686	755

It is worth emphasizing that the figures which comprise the treasury aspect are available immediately the period has ended, and are unequivocal—being simply an aggregation of transactions recorded in the cash book. It takes weeks or even

Table 2.2 Entity cash flow

	Year 2 £000	Year 3 £000
Treasury aspect		
Distributions		
Interest	310	341
Taxation	582	640
Dividends	558	614
Total	1,450	1,595
Financing		
Increased borrowings	200	220
Net cash generation	1,250	1,375
Control aspect		
Operating profit	2,250	2,475
Expansion	1,000	1,100
Net cash generation	1,250	1,375

months to apply accounting conventions (what is capital, what is revenue, what depreciation is appropriate, etc) to arrive at the figures which comprise the control aspect.

A feature of the control aspect, however, is that it can be analysed by business unit within the enterprise—but it needs to be recognized that this is a rear-view mirror approach, giving the erroneous impression that cash flow is a function of profit. The reverse is the case, as is apparent if we think of the chronological sequence of events:

☐ We have known for the best part of a year that the opening assets amounted to £11 million.

☐ Immediately the year ended, we knew that £1.375 million of cash had been generated therefrom.

☐ At that time, therefore, we knew that to the extent that our closing assets exceeded the difference, ie £9.625 million, we would have made a profit. We might call this a benchmark.

☐ A few weeks later, we established that the closing assets amounted to £12.1 million.

☐ At that precise moment, then, we knew that our profit was £2.475 million.

Looking through the front windscreen, we would observe the new information in the sequence cash flow, assets, profit: exactly the opposite sequence from that in which they are normally reported. Recalling the three Ps, we can see:

	£000
Performance as being the cash generation of	1,375
Potential as being the cost of unconsumed assets, and having increased by	1,100
Progress as being performance plus the increase in potential, implying a profit of	2,475

But this figure is clearly dependent on the accounting conventions used. Allowing for the impact of changing price levels, for example, will usually produce a higher benchmark and hence a lower profit (but will not alter that unequivocal cash flow).

More importantly, assessing potential by reference to what it is the business is attempting to maximize—the net present value of its projected cash flows—will produce quite different assessments of potential and hence a quite different quantification of progress.

THE TRIANGULAR RELATIONSHIP

It is assumed that readers will be familiar with the fundamentals of discounted cash flow, and in particular with the net present value variant. The ideas outlined in this book apply whatever the prevailing interest rates, inflation rate, risk aversion and hence the cost of capital. In order to sharpen the focus on the key issues, however, the simplifying assumption will be made that the enterprise in our worked example has a cost of capital of 15.5 per cent per annum, reflecting the interaction of 5 per cent per annum inflation and 10 per cent real.

Applying such a perception to a cash flow which just keeps up with inflation would produce a perpetuity equivalent to ten times the starting figure, as shown in Table 2.3. In other words, the inflation in the cash flow and the cost of capital

Table 2.3 Cumulative present values of inflating amounts

**Cumulative present value of £1 + 5% p.a. inflation
to be received at the end of each of a given number of years**

Year	15.5% p.a. discount factors	£1 + 5% p.a.	£ Annual present value	Cumulative present value
1	0.866	1.050	0.909	0.909
2	0.750	1.102	0.826	1.735
3	0.649	1.158	0.751	2.486
4	0.562	1.216	0.683	3.169
5	0.487	1.276	0.621	3.790
|	|	|	|	|
|	|	|	|	|
|	|	|	|	|
Infinity	Zero	Infinity	Zero	10.000

cancel out, producing the same net present value as if the real rate had been applied to the uninflated stream of income.

The logic can encompass real as well as inflationary growth. Say the income was expected to grow at five points ahead of the inflation rate, ie 10 per cent per annum, the appropriate multiple would be the inverse of a 5 per cent discount rate, ie 20; if the original income was £1,000, for example, the value would be £20,000, as shown in Table 2.4.

An important element of financial control is the articulation of figures over time. If we were to revisit the investment which forms the basis of Table 2.4 in a year's time—assuming no change in our assumptions—we would expect to value it at £1,100 × 20, ie £22,000. This could be articulated as follows:

	£
Opening value	20,000
plus cost of capital 15.5%	3,100
less cash generation	(1,100)
Benchmark	22,000
Closing net present value	22,000
Net strengthening or weakening	—

Such a focus on value and the cost of capital facilitates a continuously forward-looking approach to the monitoring of

Table 2.4 Cumulative present values of 'really growing' amounts

Cumulative present value of £1 + 10% p.a.
(in conditions of 5% p.a. inflation)
to be received at the end of each of a given number of years

Year	15.5% p.a. discount factors	£1 + 10% p.a.	£ Annual present value	Cumulative present value
1	0.866	1.100	0.952	0.952
2	0.750	1.210	0.907	1.859
3	0.649	1.331	0.864	2.723
4	0.562	1.464	0.823	3.546
5	0.487	1.611	0.784	4.330
Infinity	Zero	Infinity	Zero	20.000

strategy. Specifically, we can compare the net present value of a strategy (or business unit, or total enterprise) with a benchmark which amounts to a previous assessment, updated for the two fundamentals of financial management: the cost of capital and cash flow.

Let us revert to the example we used earlier and add in the additional assumptions that:

☐   the business's cash flows will continue to increase at 10 per cent per annum;

☐   the business's cost of capital is 15.5 per cent per annum.

On that basis, we would put its value at the end of year 2 at 20 × £1.25 million, ie £25 million, its value at the end of year 3 at 20 × £1.375 million, ie £27.5 million, and articulate these figures as follows:

	£000
Opening NPV	25,000
Cost of capital	3,875
(Cash generation)	(1,375)
Benchmark	27,500
Closing NPV	27,500
Net strengthening/weakening	–

Table 2.5 Reconciling NPV with accounts

	Historical cost accounts £000	Unrealized gains £000	Cost of capital £000	Net present value £000
Opening assets/value	11,000	14,000		25,000
			3,875	3,875
	11,000	14,000	3,875	28,875
Cash generation	1,375	–	–	1,375
Benchmark	9,625	14,000	3,875	27,500
Closing assets/value	12,100	15,400	–	27,500
Profit/net strengthening	2,475	1,400	(3,875)	–

Notice that this model is designed to return the answer zero if there has been no unexpected change in the perceived value of the investment. In practice, of course, this is a rare occurrence. The important point is that if a positive or negative number is returned, it can be thought of a variance which can be interpreted to provide accountability and feedback.

At this stage, however, it might be worth reconciling the numbers in the two models—accounting and financial management. Table 2.5 shows how this can be done.

This reconciliation is not essential, but can provide useful 'attention-directing' information. Accountants would see the closing unrealized gain, for example, as a quantification of the intangible assets of the business: the skill of the employees (thanks to training?), the reputation the business has in the market-place (thanks to advertising?), the pace of innovation (thanks to research?) and so on. Strategists, however, would see it as a quantification of the sources of competitive advantage and barriers to entry. The benefit of combining these two strands of thinking can be very considerable.

Meanwhile, for completeness, Table 2.6 shows how the treasurer might view the articulation of net present value.

These are not unrealistic assumptions, but they provide a startling message. This company, which is showing a return of 20 per cent on assets and which is maintaining its gearing while expanding five points ahead of the inflation rate, is worth more to the Inland Revenue than it is to its shareholders. The balance sheet gives the impression that the tax gatherers

Table 2.6 Attribution of value

	Borrowings £000	Taxation £000	Equity £000	Entity £000
Opening value	2,200	11,636	11,164	25,000
Cost of capital	341	1,804	1,730	3,875
	2,541	13,440	12,894	28,875
Cash generation	121	640	614	1,375
Benchmark	2,420	12,800	12,280	27,500
Closing value	2,420	12,800	12,280	27,500
Net strengthening	–	–	–	–

are the smallest of the three financial stakeholders but the cash flow shows them to be the largest. This is because of the deliberate distortion arising from taxing a version of accounting profits (unadjusted for inflation) rather than cash flow. The shareholders pay tax even on the profits which are ploughed back to generate more cash for the Revenue.

THE STRATEGIC HIERARCHY

All that has been said so far—the making and monitoring of decisions on the basis of the net present value of projected cash flows and the reconciliation of such figures with accounting numbers—can be applied at three levels:

☐ Individual dimensions of strategy. These are the basic building blocks of strategy—the product range, the location of facilities, the degrees of integration and mechanisation, etc. Within each, the choice is large and the question boils down to identifying the best.

☐ Business strategy, where we are concerned with the blending of various dimensions into a coherent business strategy. How, for example, does a top quality, high price, advertised strategy compare with a just acceptable quality, low price, unadvertised one? Usually, the number of feasible combinations is relatively small, the question being which is optimum.

☐ Corporate strategy, which is concerned with the combination of businesses into a whole, the value of which is greater than the sum of the parts. Acquisitions and divestments come into this category, with considerable attention being paid to synergies.

In each case, the competitive aspect is paramount. The value of any strategy depends on the extent to which it creates competitive advantage. There is only one way in which values can be expressed and aggregated, namely money—for, in the fullness of time, they will manifest themselves in the form of a return on investment which is satisfactory against the criterion of the cost of money.

In practice, the best place to start is with the individual dimensions, then blend them into a business strategy, then blend the business strategies into a corporate strategy. At this point it becomes possible to talk about the value of the enterprise and the sources of that value. In this way a language is developed in which strategies can be discussed, communicated and monitored throughout an organization.

It is perhaps worth stressing at this stage that the cash flow projections which are distilled into values are not objectively verifiable analyses but subjectively judgemental syntheses. They can take one of three forms, which—as in Figure 2.1—can be labelled faith, hope and expectations.

In reverse order:

☐ expectations refer to the projected results of decisions which have already been made;

☐ hope refers to the benefits which are projected to arise from decisions to be made in the foreseeable future;

☐ faith refers to the belief that opportunities will continue to present themselves beyond the horizon associated with the foreseeable future.

A growing enterprise will normally have a high proportion of its value in the faith category, whereas a shrinking one will have a high proportion in the expectations category. Over time, there needs to be a progression through the stages: faith is translated into hope, hope into expectations and expectations into results. For the cycle to continue, faith needs to be refreshed by what might be called inspiration. Traditionally,

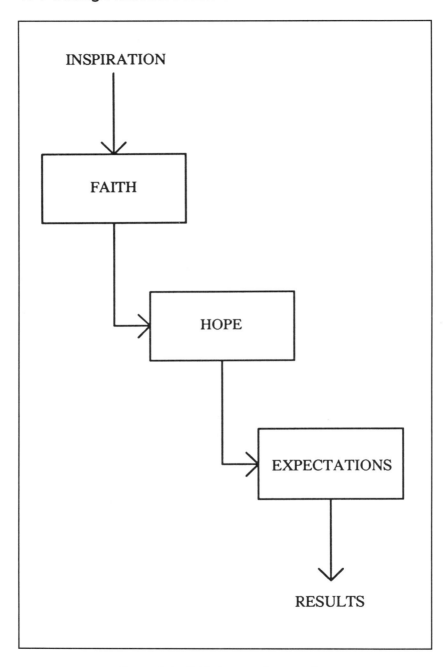

Figure 2.1 Faith, hope and expectations

accountants have concentrated on the measurement of results and on the comparison of those results with expectations. The first step beyond that is to get involved with expectations, but to do so calls for somewhat different mathematical skills: whereas the balance sheet, for example, shows the *sum* of the costs of the unconsumed tangible assets, the value of a business is the *product* of the interaction of its prevailing strategies. Accounting is essentially an arithmetic task but forecast relationships are usually expressed algebraically, and decision support often calls for differential calculus.

Preparing a budget which communicates the underlying strategies calls for different classifications from those used in accounting. Classifying outlays into capital and revenue, then subdividing the latter into fixed and variable costs, for example, reflects a short-term focus. The financial manager will want to classify them in a way which reflects the relationships: price/volume, volume/cost and inertia. Specifically, outlays will need to be classified under such headings as volume responsive, volume anticipative, volume inducing, volume sustaining or regenerative, and the financial manager will want to attach to each a value based on the projected benefits. These can be related by means of a strategic map, a generic version of which appears as Figure 2.2.

REACTIONS

The idea that value is a function of cash generating potential has been around for some time and is well understood by anyone with a grounding in economics. Intellectually, therefore, it is a small step forward to articulate opening and closing perceptions of net present value. However, many accountants have difficulty with the theory because it cannot be confined within the additive matrix with which they are familiar.

In the same way, the quantification of subjective judgements about the future does not come easily to those reared on the task of searching for the one objectively verifiable truth about the past, even though there is some discomfort with the recognition that both accounting in industry and auditing in public practice are passive activities. The answer is to

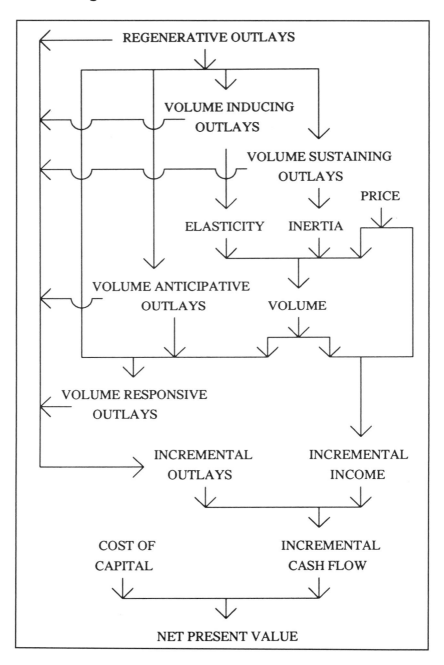

Figure 2.2 Interrelationships

recognize that accountancy consists of more than accounting and auditing; in particular, it embraces forward-looking, proactive financial management.

The fact is that managers are making decisions based on their subjective judgements all the time. There is every reason to consolidate these judgements into the only common language—money—so that they might be evaluated and monitored. Most importantly, they need to be related to the criterion of viability in a modern economy: the time value of money. Significantly, non-financial managers find that they can relate to the idea of justifying proposals along the lines of projected cash flows, without the unnecessary complications of concepts of capital and revenue, profits and assets. Naturally they welcome, but initially can be disorientated by, questions from the finance function such as 'Are you sure you have built enough flexibility into your plant specification?' or 'Are you sure we should not be spending more on marketing?' The only negatives are conflicts with messages emanating from top management in terms of keeping expenditure within budget, delivering the promised profit figure and so on.

In many respects, the audience which provides the most worrying reaction is the top management of publicly quoted companies. They frequently argue that they personally 'cannot afford to be forward looking and long-termist when the capital market is backward looking and short-termist'. Share prices are seen by many to be a function of reported profits (or at best forecast profits for the current year). Should profits be consciously reduced by investments in research, development or marketing, they argue, the share price will fall and their security jeopardized by action from institutional shareholders or by a takeover. The predator, it is argued, would simply strip out enough revenue investment in order to deliver short-term profits and the consequent increase in his share price would enable him to offer his paper for even more acquisitions, thus providing an engine of growth. Forward-looking companies, on this analysis, are likely to be gobbled up by backward-looking ones. Bad money drives out good.

The problem is intensified by the tendency for annual reports and meetings to be dominated by consideration of backward-looking accounting numbers. Those active in the capital market blame the lack of forward-looking information for their own short-termism. Consider how much more effective corporate governance would be if:

- □ financial reports encompassed the monitoring of strategic progress against the criterion of maximizing cash generating potential;

- □ company chairmen concentrated on forward-looking issues in their public pronouncements and gave an indication, for example, of the rate of dividend growth they believe their strategies will sustain;

- □ analysts and financial journalists were to focus on companies' cash generating potential and their cost of capital, and thereby reach judgements on their long-term health.

Strategic financial management is designed primarily for executives concerned to manage their enterprises for long-term financial success. That task would be made easier by the provision of more meaningful information to their various stakeholders. In the process, the 'expectation gap' which continues to bother the accountancy profession world-wide would be narrowed significantly.

Pricing

A key control point in any strategy is pricing. In this chapter we look at the relationship between prices, volumes and costs, and see how the optimum can be identified. On to this is grafted what used to be meant by 'goodwill', ie the tendency for satisfied customers to come back for more, in order to arrive at the longer term value of a particular policy. We also see how to establish a benchmark against which progress can be monitored.

THE MATHEMATICS OF FINANCIAL MANAGEMENT

Chapter 1 described control and accountability in terms of comparing what happens with what was forecast to happen at the time a decision was made. The corresponding information systems were referred to as monitoring, forecasting (sub-divided into relationship and expected outcome versions) and decision support. We now turn to the ways in which these various kinds of information are quantified.

Monitoring systems in general, and the accounting model in particular, are couched in terms which can be accommodated by simple arithmetic. The balance sheet, for example, consists of the sum of the costs of the tangible assets of the organization at a point in time, while the profit statement shows revenue minus costs. Behind those statements are such things as stock valuations, arrived at by multiplying a quantity by a unit cost.

The very expression 'relationship forecasts', however, signals a need for the greater power of algebra. The expression 'decision support', likewise, suggests the optimization process for which differential calculus is appropriate. People who have devoted a high proportion of their time to the accounting task, but who are now called upon to be financial managers, would be well advised to revise the knowledge of quantitative techniques they needed at the earlier stages of professional examinations.

For what financial managers often need to do is to take the judgements of their colleagues as to relationships and express them algebraically so that the various options can be evaluated. The more use that is made of the power of the computer, the more this skill is required. Pricing provides a good starting point for putting it into practice.

It is useful to have on file a general purpose price/volume relationship which can be pictured graphically as a line which slopes downwards from left to right. The discussion with colleagues is then geared to putting some scales to the graph. Let us start with a simple example of a consultant who reckons that:

☐   if he charged £150 per day for his time, he would have enough business to occupy 350 days of the year;

☐   the higher the charge, the lower the volume of business, to the point that if he charged £1,200 per day, he would not attract any business;

☐   between those two extremes, the relationship is linear, eg a half-way price of £675 would induce a half-way volume of 175 days work.

How do we express this relationship in a form in which it can be input to a decision, eg the price to charge if the objective is to maximize income? The first step is to relate the range of £1,050 across the charging scale to the range of 350 days work across the volume scale, ie a ratio (or slope of the line) of 3:1. Combining this with the view that the scale starts at a price of £150, which generates 350 days work, we can quantify the consultant's judgement as follows:

$$Number\ of\ days\ work = 350 - (price\ in\ £ - 150)/3$$

$$= 400 - price/3$$

and put scales to the graph as shown in Figure 3.1.

The next step is to consider aggregate revenue. At a price of

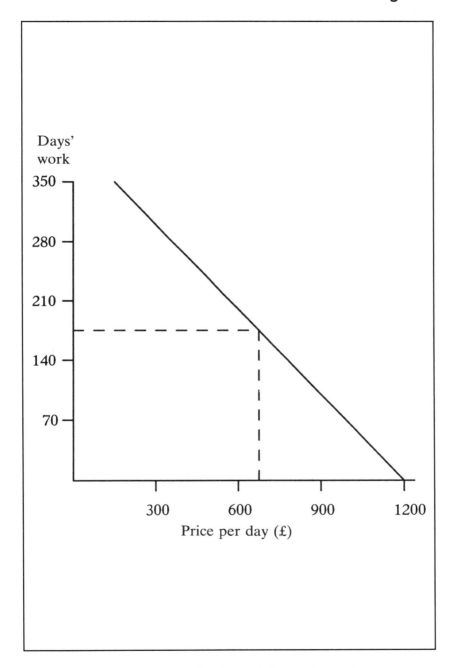

Figure 3.1 Consultant's price/volume relationship

£150 per day, the volume is 350 days, for a total revenue of £52,500. Doubling the price to £300 per day would reduce the demand to 300 days, for a total revenue of £90,000. Clearly, this aggregate will increase up to a certain point before starting to fall to the zero associated with a price of £1,200 per day. The shape of this graph is as shown in Figure 3.2 but what is the price at the point where revenue is maximized, ie at which the curve turns downwards?

To identify this point, we need to develop an algebraic expression for revenue, as follows:

$$\text{If } volume = 400 - price/3$$

$$\text{then } revenue = price \, (400 - price/3)$$

$$\text{or, algebraically, } r = 400p - p^2/3$$

This is where differential calculus, which focuses on the rate of change, comes into its own. It tells us that the gradient of this curve at any point (dr/dp in mathematical form) can be expressed as $400 - 2p/3$. At the point at which revenue is maximized, the gradient is zero, ie $400 - 2p/3 = 0$. This is where $p = 600$, ie where price = £600 per day, volume 200 days, and revenue £120,000. We can check this by evaluating the revenue either side of the maximum:

$$price = 540, \, volume = 220, \, revenue = 118,800$$

$$price = 660, \, volume = 180, \, revenue = 118,800$$

There was a time when management accountants were seen as being the experts in costing. In particular, they were seen as having the skills necessary to identify and assemble the information required by those who effectively made the trade-off between price and volume. This trade-off might take the form of quoting a firm price for a particular line of business and accepting the consequences in terms of volume, or deciding that a particular line of business was worth having at a price determined by others, eg customers or competitors. Either way, a key piece of information was the consequences of a given volume in terms of cost and investment.

For many, no doubt, this is still the case. All too often, however, qualified accountants with job titles like financial

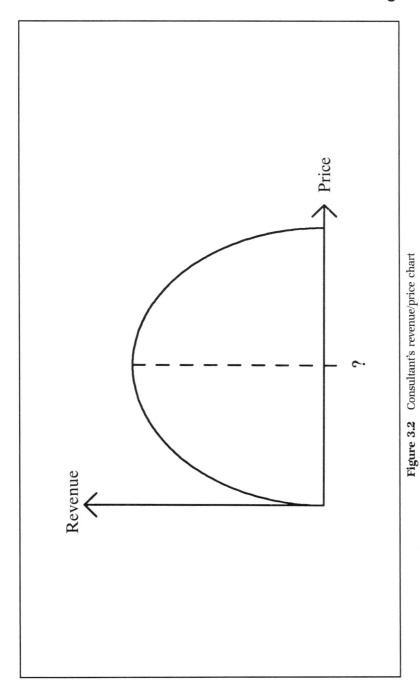

Figure 3.2 Consultant's revenue/price chart

controller say that they do not get involved in matters of pricing—these are left to sales, marketing or general management colleagues. What such colleagues are using in place of relevant costs is not clear, but unless they have their own separate information systems, problems are bound to arise.

For most businesses, pricing is the dominant area of managerial discretion. Other dimensions of strategy may be in perfect working order, but if your pricing is wrong your chances of survival are very restricted. You need to be familiar with the language of pricing, eg:

☐ A 'penetration' policy aimed at getting a high market share and discouraging competition. The Japanese electronic manufacturers have usually adopted this approach. A severe form is 'predatory' pricing aimed at eliminating one or more competitors.

☐ A 'prestige' policy aimed at getting very high margins on a small share of the market—the Rolls-Royce approach. A weaker form is 'premium' pricing in which, for example, the benefits of having branded a product are taken in the form of a higher price rather than higher volume.

☐ A 'skimming' policy which means starting with a high price but being prepared to reduce it as time goes by. Hardback books followed by paperback versions are a good example.

☐ 'Distress pricing', ie charging what the market will bear in adverse conditions. It is worth recalling the plumbers' principle, ie that the value of a service is at its greatest just before it is performed: always agree the price while the kitchen is flooded.

Clearly, what is the best approach will vary from product to product and over the product lifecycle. The role of the financial management member of the team will be to quantify the judgements of more knowledgeable colleagues, in a form which concludes: 'If you're right about the relationship between price and volume, then the optimum price is . . .'

There are two stages to understanding this process: one focuses on this year's contribution, the second on the longer-term effect.

MAXIMIZING CONTRIBUTION

Maximizing contribution means getting the right balance between price, volume and volume responsive costs. Say, for example, that those in closest contact with the market estimate that the relationship between the volume of sales this year and the price charged is summed up in the expression:

$$Volume = 8,000 + 4\ (3,000 - price\ in\ £\ per\ unit)$$

If volume responsive costs are £2,000 per unit, what price optimizes contribution? As with the consultancy example, some people might be inclined towards a trial and error approach. Others—in the ascendancy—would use a spread-sheet, which has the added advantage of facilitating a graphical representation. To short cut the exercise, we can use differential calculus again, as follows:

Let price	$= x$
Volume	$= 20,000 - 4x$
Unit contribution	$= £(x - 2,000)$
Aggregate contribution	$= £(28,000x - 4x^2 - 40\ \text{million})$
Maximized where $\quad 8x$	$= 28,000$
Optimum price therefore	$= £3,500$
Volume at that price	$= 6,000$
Unit contribution	$= £1,500$
Aggregate contribution	$= £9\ \text{million}$

The relationships assumed in this evaluation are linear, but it is equally possible to use curvilinear ones. Indeed, forced to express the relationship between price and volume for their products, many managers today would produce something like line A in Figure 3.3. If they were to try to increase the price by a penny, they reckon, they would lose all their volume; if they were to reduce their prices by a penny, so would their competitors and everybody would be worse off.

But what does this boxed-in situation tell the strategist? It says that the company is selling a commodity—a product which is indistinguishable from that offered by the competitors. It says that the company has no distinctive competence, no competitive advantage unless it happens to be the lowest cost producer

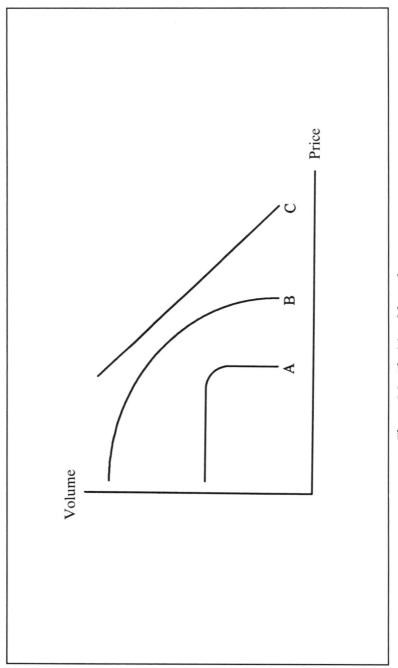

Figure 3.3 Elasticity of demand

by a significant margin. For all but that one company in the market, there are basically only two directions in which to go. One is to carry on and accept the inevitable decline, shrinking to the point of extinction. There is no more to be said about this, other than it has been a depressingly common phenomenon in the UK in recent years.

The other is to think about what is necessary to move the curve north-eastwards and get its shape closer to the diagonal, eg to line B in Figure 3.3. Specifically, this calls for the identification of some points of distinction. These may be associated with the quality of the product—eg a longer life, greater reliability, less maintenance or closer tailoring to the customers' needs. Alternatively, they may be associated with the quality of the service offered, eg a just-in-time delivery to the point of use or a helpful after-sales service.

Beyond that, further progress—say to line C—is likely to require an investment in communication with customers and potential customers, eg advertising. Substantial investments in improving the quality of the product and the related service are unlikely to pay off unless potential customers know about them. Note, however, that the benefit still depends on pricing. What advertising does is allow you to sell more at the same price or the same at a higher price (or some combination in between). We shall explore this topic in the next chapter, but note that you still have to choose where on the price/volume line you want to be.

INERTIA

The evaluation we carried out above focused on contribution in the current year in order to provide us with a simple, rolling start to our worked examples. We now need to pick up one of the points which differentiates financial management from accounting, namely the need to think beyond the end of the current financial year.

To do this we need to embrace the concept of inertia, the tendency for things to carry on as they are—or at least in proportion to how they are. Perhaps the best starting point is with the recognition that satisfied customers are likely to come back for more. In the long run, the extent to which they come

Table 3.1 Evaluation I

| Year | Factor | £000 | |
		Absolute	Discounted
1	0.866	9,000	7,794
2	0.750	4,725	3,543
3	0.649	2,481	1,611
4	0.561	1,302	732
etc	etc	etc	333
			151
			69
			31
			14
			6
			3
			1
			14,288

back for more will depend on a number of factors, such as the quality of the product or the effectiveness of the sales force. These factors will be examined in later chapters. At a point in time, however, the extent of this inertia will be determined by current attitudes.

Say that it is believed that—for the product in our pricing example—there is a 50 per cent chance of satisfied customers coming back next year. Thus, on the basis of events and decisions already made, if the volume is to be 6,000 this year, there will be a consequent 3,000 next year, 1,500 the year after that, and so on. Assuming, as in Chapter 2, 5 per cent inflation and a real cost of capital of 10 per cent per annum (ie a nominal cost of capital of 15.5 per cent per annum), we can assess the 'expectations' (as opposed to hope or faith) component of the value of this business to be £14,288 million, as shown in Table 3.1.

This is the value of the chosen pricing policy. Again, it might be useful to have the information on a spreadsheet so that the sensitivity of this value to the pricing decision, to the volume responsive costs and to the extent of the inertia can be graphically displayed. Such a representation can also clarify managers' understanding of the dynamics: some may be surprised, for example, to find that the optimum price is quite independent of the extent of the inertia—thus helping to determine the shape of the strategic map mentioned in the previous chapter.

Another useful pointer concerns the time-scale of the evaluations necessary for strategic financial management. Notice how, thanks to a combination of the fall off in volume and the discounting of cash flows, 98 per cent of the value is in the first five years—a popular time-scale for many strategic reviews or so-called 'long-range plans'.

MONITORING

Decision-making is perhaps the most important element of control but we must not forget the need to monitor what happens thereafter. The logic of benchmarking, introduced in Chapter 2, is equally applicable to any aspect of strategy. Assuming, for the time being, that things work out as expected and that the judgement as to the later years remains unchanged, we can establish a benchmark against which to monitor the progress of this product as follows:

	£000
Opening net present value	14,288
Cost of capital 15.5%	2,215
Cash (generation)	(9,000)
Benchmark	7,503

This could be confirmed—though as confidence in the approach increases, it should be not be necessary—by rerunning the evaluation from year 2 onwards, as shown in Table 3.2.

In practice, this will rarely happen, of course. Changes in perceptions will affect the forward view but the variance between the new evaluation and the benchmark will provide accountability and feedback. Other decisions will also have an impact, as we shall see in subsequent chapters.

Table 3.2 One year on

Year	Factor	£000 Absolute	£000 Discounted
1	0.866	4,725	4,091
2	0.750	2,481	1,860
3	0.649	1,302	846
4	0.561	683	384
etc	etc	etc	176
			79
			36
			17
			7
			3
			2
			1
			7,503

Volume Inducing Outlays

In a rapidly changing environment, competitive strength is increasingly associated with the very investments which the accounting model dismisses as intangible. In this chapter, we look at one such investment—marketing—and see how it can be evaluated, optimised and monitored. Along the way, misconceptions surrounding the debate as to the inclusion of brands on balance sheets are exposed.

GENERIC STRATEGIES

Recent years have seen an outpouring of literature on the subject of identifying possible strategies. Usually, however, the literature stops short of explaining how the various possibilities can be evaluated and the optimum chosen. Filling this vacuum presents a significant opportunity for the finance function.

Many (but not all) strategies are concerned with the stance of a business *vis-à-vis* its customers and competitors. One of the key choices which has to be made is whether to aim to be the lowest cost producer in an industry or to seek to differentiate what is offered from the competition. The latter course is usually associated with the concept of 'branding' —a concept the popularity of which seems to go in cycles.

In the UK, for example, the 1970s saw a significant retreat from branding. Manufacturers of fast moving consumer goods were faced with rapidly escalating costs (remember threshold agreements?) but prevented from recovering them in selling prices (remember the Price Commission?). As a consequence, cost minimization was given priority, which for many businesses meant range rationalization and the supply of goods bearing retailers' 'own labels'. The latter have since become strong brands in their own right—consumers trust the leading retailers to control quality and value for money.

The 1980s saw a resurgence of interest in brands, not least because of the attention given to their value in the context of published accounts, especially the 'goodwill on acquisition' aspect. That episode muddied the waters in a way which will be described later in this chapter, but it is worth pausing to consider why there was such a flurry of interest in 'old' brands as opposed to building new ones. The consumer's demand for greater variety, but with reassurance as to quality, etc, and the capability of flexible manufacturing systems to respond were important, but other factors which had a bearing were:

□ The balance of supply and demand in the industries and markets concerned. To launch new brands in an industry where capacity is already adequate (and expanding as technology advances) would be to risk dragging down the profitability of the whole industry. This is doubly so in a European context: it is not feasible for all the national brands to become Continental ones. Mergers of established businesses seem to make more sense at both micro and macro levels of economics.

□ The cost of branding. The cost of advertising has increased substantially in real terms in recent years. This may ease as more television channels become operational but, at the moment, reinforcing an established brand looks to be much cheaper than launching a new one. Extending a brand across several products is particularly attractive, in that it provides reassurance to the consumer, while offering greater variety.

□ The time needed to reap economies of scale. The economics of selling, distribution and administration have improved enormously, making it possible to increase volume throughput with very small increases in cost. If such opportunities can be exploited quickly, they are more likely to justify the investment against the criterion of the cost of capital.

Some aspects of these pressures will be dealt with in later

chapters; in the remainder of this one, we shall focus on the most obvious aspect of branding: advertising.

BRANDS ON THE BALANCE SHEET

In some countries of the world—Japan and Germany, for example—published accounts are seen as essentially legalistic documents. They provide the main input to taxation computations, and they determine how much profit is distributable. In the UK, however, published accounts are put to additional uses. In particular, they provide the basis for denominating directors' freedom to act. In articles of association, borrowing agreements and Stock Exchange listing documents, the size of an acquisition or new borrowing which can be initiated without prior approval from the shareholder is limited to a defined percentage of the net assets shown on the balance sheet.

In the feverish takeover atmosphere of the late 1980s, a number of observers (some of whom should have known better) professed amazement that businesses were being bought and sold at prices which bore no relation to their net assets as shown on the balance sheet. Such net assets were, of course, limited to those of a tangible variety—property, equipment, stocks and debtors. It is interesting to observe that to the strategist, these items are more likely to appear as liabilities to be minimized. Key inputs to competitive advantage, in a rapidly changing environment, are more likely to be of the intangible variety.

This conundrum created particular problems for the boards of acquisitive UK quoted companies, since they were required to write off goodwill on acquisition against current year profits. The more they acquired, the lower their net worth became and the less freedom the directors would have. Some observers would see this as a desirable feature of corporate governance, but it is easy to see why the directors concerned didn't. A number of them therefore decided to rewrite some basic accounting conventions.

The most blatant move was made by the directors of Ranks Hovis McDougall plc, who asserted that 'a balance sheet purports to show the underlying strength of the business'.

Having thus chosen to disregard SSAP 2, they employed Interbrand plc, who expressed their opinion that RHM's home-grown brands were worth £678 million, duly added this to their net worth and made a takeover bid which would have been beyond their powers had they not augmented the balance sheet.

The Institute of Chartered Accountants sponsored some research by a team from the London Business School, who reported back quickly and clearly to the effect that:

☐ brands undoubtedly have economic value, but in most cases it is impossible to separate it from the rest of the business;

☐ any assessment of value involves subjective judgements about the future, which cannot be accommodated within the objectivity which is a feature of published accounts;

☐ unless they disclose new information, brand valuations are of no significance except as a signal of management insecurity or aggressive intent;

☐ bankers and analysts assess financial strength by references to cash flow, interest cover, etc, not to balance sheets;

☐ the absence of empirical verification of valuations throws into question the willingness of auditors to accept them;

☐ the then (and still, at the time of writing) position is potentially corrosive to the whole basis of financial reporting;

☐ to allow brands, whether acquired or home grown, to be included in balance sheets is highly unwise.

The Stock Exchange has condoned and encouraged the continuation of the practice, the accountancy profession has continued to prevaricate on the issue (which may or may not be connected with the fact that a number of firms are earning substantial fees from valuations and their audit) and the Accounting Standards setters appear to be worried that a clear banning of brand valuations would run into problems of acceptability to powerful boards of directors.

Meanwhile, however, it is worth noting that no examples

have been traced of companies which put brand valuations into their management accounts or measures of performance. It is something which is done on consolidation of financial accounts, ie debit brand valuation, credit reserves, with no impact on the profit statement. Indeed, it is rare for the valuations to be updated or any opinion expressed as to whether they have grown stronger or weaker. In short, putting brands on the balance sheet has nothing to offer financial managers and needs to be consciously disregarded.

A TALE OF TWO STRATEGIES

At the strategic level, decisions are predominantly about trade-offs between cash flow now and later, or between current profit and future growth. Choosing a branding strategy (as distinct, say, from providing 'own label' goods) will usually mean lower profit and cash generation in the short term, in the expectation of a higher rate of growth over time.

Table 4.1 compares two strategies, A and B, first in terms of accounting numbers and then in terms of net present values. A is an unbranded strategy which produces a cash flow of £1.865 million, expected to increase in line with inflation, and B is a branded strategy which produces a cash flow of £1.250 million, expected to grow five points ahead of inflation. Making our usual assumptions of 5 per cent inflation and a real cost of capital of 10 per cent per annum (ie a nominal 15.5 per cent per annum) the two strategies are worth £18.650 million and £25.000 million respectively.

If the only language in which strategies are discussed is that of the accounting model, there has to be a danger that strategy A will be preferred. It shows higher profits and return on assets, and higher cash generation. The language of strategic financial management, on the other hand, would say that if you believe the projected growth, strategy B is preferable. There is considerable circumstantial evidence to say that UK managers' preoccupation with accounting numbers is a contributory factor to their unwillingness to invest in market-building strategies to the extent their German and Japanese competitors do.

It might be concluded that the value of branding, in this case, is the difference between the two valuations, ie £25.000

Table 4.1 A tale of two strategies

Assumption Cost of capital 15.5% (10% real, 5% inflation)		
Strategy	*A*	*B*
Real growth rate	zero	5% p.a.
Annuity multiple	10	20
£000, Increasing with inflation		
Year 2		
Opening assets	10,000	10,000
Closing assets	10,500	11,000
(Expansion)	(500)	(1,000)
Profit	2,365	2,250
Cash flow	1,865	1,250
£000 Strategic evaluation, Year 3		
Opening npv	18,650	25,000
Cost of capital	2,891	3,875
(Cash flow)	(1,958)	(1,375)
Benchmark	19,583	27,500
Closing npv	19,583	27,500
Net strengthening	–	–

million − £18.650 million = £6.350 million. It would clearly be meaningless, however, to add this to the tangible assets of £11.000 million, producing an aggregate of £17.350 million. Although accountants might like to think that the value of the business is the sum of its tangible and intangible assets, the reality is that value is independent of tangible assets: the dependent variable is the figure for intangibles—in this case a total of £14.000 million, corresponding with the unrealized gains figure we saw in Table 2.5.

EVALUATION OF INVESTMENT

Branding is about identification and differentiation. In some cases, the differentiation is between products emanating from the same producer—as with various individually branded lagers, for example. In others, it is between a wide range of products emanating from competing manufacturers—as with baked beans or soup. In still others, the two may be combined—a product within a house name, like Cadbury's Crunchie.

There are certain generalizations which can be made, however. Perhaps the most fundamental is that branding is about reassurance and the reduction of uncertainty. It provides customers with a reassurance, ahead of purchase, that the goods or services will be of a standard in line with that previously experienced. This is particularly noticeable where the product is not actually seen or is not capable of testing by the customer—as with petrol, for example. Branding provides an identity within which to develop other elements of the marketing mix, such as promotions.

For the supplier, branding is expected to make demand more predictable, with consequent cost benefits, and to provide a rallying point for management and employees. But most of all, it is expected to improve the shape of the demand curve. We saw in Chapter 3 how, at a point in time, the relationship between price and volume was essentially fixed. Over time, however, it is possible to move the curve to the right and/or make it less convex, thereby providing an opportunity to sell more volume at the same price or achieve a higher price for the same volume than would otherwise be the case. Figure 4.1 shows this graphically.

At the risk of labouring the obvious, note that the extent of the movement is not an objectively verifiable measurement; it a subjectively judgmental assessment produced by those closest to the action—usually the marketing manager responsible for the brand. What the financial manager seeks to do is to translate this assessment into an expression which will facilitate the identification of the optimum point. To see how this might work, let us return to the pricing example, where the relationship between price and volume is summed up in the expression:

Volume = 8,000 + 4(3,000 − price in £ per unit).

Given a volume responsive outlay of £2,000 per unit, we identified the optimum price as £3,500, which produced a contribution of £9 million this year.

To evaluate, say, a 10 per cent shift in the demand curve (10 per cent more volume at any given price) we would proceed as follows:

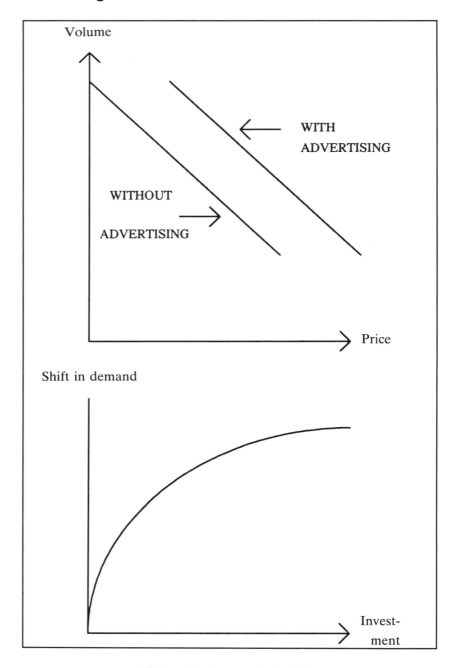

Figure 4.1 Impact of advertising

Let price	$= x$
Volume now	$= 22{,}000 - 4.4x$
Unit contribution is still	$= \pounds(x - 2{,}000)$
Aggregate contribution now	$= \pounds(30{,}800x - 4.4x^2 - 44$ million)
Maximized where $\qquad 8.8x$	$= 30{,}800$
Optimum price, therefore, still	$= \pounds 3{,}500$
Volume at that price	$= 6{,}600$
Unit contribution still	$= \pounds 1{,}500$
Aggregate contribution now	$= \pounds 9.9$ million

Notice how—provided the gradient of the line remains the same—the price remains unchanged. Had the gradient changed, a different optimum price would have emerged. Readers might like to practise their mathematical skills by re-running the calculations on the assumption, for example, that the relationship shifts to one summed up in the expression:

$$Volume = 8{,}000 + 3.6 \ (3{,}000 - price \ in \ \pounds \ per \ unit)$$

In this case, the optimum price and the resulting contribution would be higher, though the volume would be lower.

There are basically two ways in which the relationship between advertising investment and the shift in the demand curve can be expressed:

☐ in the form of a curve, as shown in Figure 4.2—in which case differential calculus continues to be appropriate;

☐ in the form of a series of feasible scenarios, as discussed in the example which follows and illustrated in Figure 4.2.

Let us imagine that the original price/volume relationship had been arrived at against the background of a budgeted investment in advertising of £1.6 million (ie a net contribution of £7.4 million at the optimum price, implying a net present value of £14.288 million — £1.600 million/1.155, ie £12.903 million on the assumption of 50 per cent per annum inertia associated with the product). Freeing oneself from this practice (of spending what has been budgeted, probably on the basis of past spending or a percentage of sales) can often provide the breakthrough to the adoption of a strategic

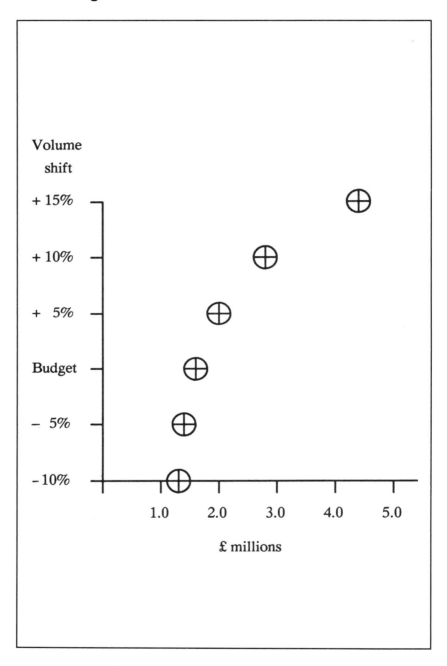

Figure 4.2 Volume/advertising investment

approach to financial management. The marketing manager may need to be prompted to say what he or she thinks would happen at different levels of investment.

Say, for example, he or she believed that:

1   Without any advertising, this year's volume would be 10 per cent lower than budget. At this level, contribution would be £8.100 million and net present value £12.859 million.

2   As a consequence of fixed production costs of £1.300 million, the minimum investment required to have any significant impact on demand is £1.400 million (present value £1.212 million), at which level volume would be 5 per cent lower than budget. This would suggest a gross contribution of 95 per cent of £9.000 million, ie £8.550 million, a gross present value of 95 per cent of £14.288 million, ie £13.574 million, and therefore a net present value of £12.362 million.

3   Increasing the investment to £2.000 million (present value £1.732 million) would increase this year's volume by 5 per cent. This would suggest a gross contribution of £9.450 million, a gross present value of £15.002 million, and therefore a net present value of £13.270 million.

4   Increasing the investment to £2.800 million (present value £2.425 million) would increase this year's volume by 10 per cent. This would suggest a gross contribution of £9.900 million, a gross present value of £15.717 million, and therefore a net present value of £13.292 million.

5   Increasing the investment to £4.400 million (present value £3.810 million) would increase this year's volume by 15 per cent. This would suggest a gross contribution of £10.350 million, a gross present value of £16.431 million, and therefore a net present value of £12.621 million.

On this basis, as is clear from Table 4.2, the conclusion would be to increase the advertising investment by £1.200 to £2.800 million. Compared with the budget, this would increase gross contribution by £0.9 million and net present value by £0.389 million. Note, however, that net contribution this year will be reduced by £0.300 million. Here we have a clear conflict between what is good for the long-term health of the business

Table 4.2 Optimizing volume inducing outlays

| £000 | | | | £000 | |
V/I outlay	Present value	Volume	Contri-bution	Present value	NPV
–	–	5,400	8,100	12,858	12,859
1,400	1,212	5,700	8,550	13,574	12,362
1,600	1,385	6,000	9,000	14,288	12,903
2,000	1,732	6,300	9,450	15,002	13,270
2,800	2,425	6,600	9,900	15,717	13,292
4,400	3,810	6,900	10,350	16,431	12,621

and what is good for this year's reported profits. It has to be acknowledged that some businesses would choose to sub-optimize, eg restrict the investment to £2.000 million: this falls short of maximum net present value but protects current profits.

Alternatively, we might say that the value of the advertising is the difference between 3) and 1), that is £13.292 million − £12.859 million = £0.433 million.

FORECAST OUTCOME AND BENCHMARKING

To relate this to the elements of control introduced in Chapter 1, we have input forecast relationships (elasticity of demand, cost/volume, advertising/elasticity) into a decision-support process and concluded that the optimum investment for the product in question is £2.8 million. Assuming this decision is implemented, the next step is to log the expected outcome, as summarized in Table 4.3.

Again, as with earlier examples, we can start the bench-marking process. If our assumptions remain the same, we should expect the business to be worth £8.252 million in a year's time, as follows:

	£000
Opening net present value	13,292
Cost of capital 15.5%	2,060
(Cash generation)	(7,100)
Closing net present value	8,252

Table 4.3 Evaluation II

		£000	
Year	Factor	Absolute	Discounted
1	0.866	7,100	6,149
2	0.750	5,197	3,898
3	0.649	2,728	1,771
4	0.561	1,432	805
etc	etc	etc	366
			166
			76
			34
			16
			7
			3
			1
			13,292

Table 4.4 One year on

		£000	
Year	Factor	Absolute	Discounted
1	0.866	5,197	4,501
2	0.750	2,728	2,046
3	0.649	1,432	930
4	0.561	752	423
etc	etc	etc	192
			87
			40
			18
			8
			4
			2
			1
			8,252

This can be checked in the usual way by recalculating the individual years' cash flows as shown in Table 4.4.

Bear in mind that these examples have, thus far, only looked at the interaction of advertising investment and pricing. Volume responsive costs and inertia were held at the original assumptions. We now need to relax these assumptions and see how any changes can be evaluated.

Volume Anticipative Outlays

All businesses seem to be experiencing a shift away from costs which are directly attributable to products and/or are responsive to volume change towards those which are shared across products and/or are incurred in anticipation of volume throughput. Financial managers are rarely concerned with the question of how to apportion these costs, after the event, to products. They are, however, concerned with the appropriate level of such costs. In this chapter, we see how such a decision is approached, evaluated and monitored.

SYMPTOMS AND PRESSURES

One of the megatrends we identified in the first chapter was that evidenced by a steady reduction in the proportion of costs which are directly associated with particular products or customers, and which tend to vary according to the volume of products or customers. Conversely, there has been an increase in the proportion of costs which are shared across products or customers, and which tend to be insensitive to volume changes.

Technological developments are often the root cause of this trend. Mechanization is an obvious example, particularly the adoption of flexible supply systems designed to meet customers' expectations in terms of tailoring what is offered to their specific needs, including the product specification and the speed of response. The costs incurred irrespective of volume—such as having engineers standing by to change tools as and when necessary, or deal with breakdowns—will be higher, but the incremental cost associated with volume throughput will be lower. The growing popularity of measuring team (as opposed to individual) performance has reinforced the trend, as has that towards intangibles (eg investments in training), producing a sharp increase in the proportion of costs classified as overheads in the accounting model.

The word 'overheads' has pejorative overtones, conjuring up an image of costs which need to be minimized. Nothing could be further from the truth: in a rapidly changing environment, competitive advantage is increasingly associated with investments which are intangible and costs which are indirect and/or fixed. This has given rise to problems as far as costing systems are concerned, the most publicized of responses collecting in two main camps: throughput accounting and activity based costing (ABC). Which you prefer will be influenced by your attitude towards apportionments.

Apportionments are essential to financial accounting, for use in stock 'valuation' and in the analysis of profits by business segment. A long time ago, however, adherents of the marginal costing school argued that that was not how profits were made. In reality, products make contributions (sales minus variable costs) to a pool from which fixed costs are defrayed. If, in aggregate, contribution exceeds fixed costs, the business shows a profit; if not, a loss.

One of the most powerful applications of the technique was the use of 'contribution per unit of limiting factor' as the basis for decision-making, eg pricing and choices between alternative production schedules. If a piece of plant was a bottleneck, for example, giving priority to those products which showed the highest contribution per minute of use of that plant would lead to the maximization of profit.

Throughput accounting is a descendant of marginal costing, though its advocates like to highlight 'focal points' (eg core technologies which distinguish the enterprise) rather than short-term constraints. Throughput is defined, effectively, as added value, ie sales minus material costs, and is related to the passage of time, eg throughput per minute of focal point capacity.

Use of any variation on the marginal costing theme has been incompatible with financial accounts since the introduction of SSAP 9, which prohibits its use for stock valuations. This is a serious problem given the high proportion of accounts which are 'integrated', ie which position management accounts as a subset of financial accounts. Most worrying has been the activity based costing bandwagon, which starts from the observation that the costs which are used for stock valuations are not suitable for making decisions.

Brushing aside protestations that no one had ever claimed they were, this school of thought has developed more sophisticated (ie multistage) techniques of apportionment. The essence of these techniques is the idea that costs are caused by activities (eg set-ups), the extent of the need for which are determined by cost drivers (eg the number of set-ups). Costs are first collected under the headings of relevant activities and then apportioned to products according to the drivers. If the total cost of setting up, for example, was £1 million last year, and there were 20,000 set-ups, each product would bear a cost equivalent to £50 per set-up.

The resulting 'activity based' costs differ from those used in financial accounts, of course, and you are asked to believe that:

☐   as they are different from the costs you agreed were irrelevant, they must be relevant (a spurious argument but one which was sustained for a surprisingly long time, it will be recalled, by those attempting to impose current cost accounting);

☐   they can be regarded as the true costs, the only accurate costs, the real costs (different consultants like to use different adjectives). The fact that they ignore the cost/volume relationship and are true to only one particular volume scenario (that which applied at some time in the past) rules them out, however, for anyone wishing to look forward and choose between feasible alternatives.

A key question for many organizations relates to the purpose of costing: is it primarily an element within the accounting model or is it an element within financial management? If the former, then the simpler and cheaper the costing system, the better: activity based costs would be wasteful. If the latter, then concepts like truth and accuracy will have to be subordinated to that of relevance: one of the leading advocates of ABC has acknowledged that it is 'designed not to produce decision relevant information'. If anything can be singled out as 'causing' costs, it is decision-making.

It is unlikely that one system can satisfy both sets of needs, increasing the pressure to separate financial management from accounting. Businesses which have expanded by acquisition abroad have learned how varied are the approaches to cost apportionment. Often the problem emerges when a decision has to be made about where to locate a particular piece of new plant. Beware of falling into the trap of embarking on a project to standardize costing around the group: if you ever manage it, it will be too late and will still only look backwards. Decisions should be based on forecasts of cash flows, discounted at the cost of capital.

FROM TACTICS TO STRATEGY

On the basis of the observations above, it seems clear that—as far as the operational and tactical levels of control are concerned—the logic of direct/marginal costing is most appropriate:

☐ Costs are collected according to responsibility, so that each level of management can look at revenues and costs which they can control themselves.

☐ Product profitability is viewed in terms of sales minus costs directly attributable to those products.

☐ If one factory makes a number of products, its profitability is viewed in terms of aggregate factory contribution minus shared factory costs.

☐ If the output of several factories is sold through one sales force, then the profitability of this 'business unit' can be viewed in terms of aggregate factory contribution minus shared selling costs.

☐ If a number of business units share such services as physical distribution, invoicing, sales ledger, credit control, etc, the profit of the total enterprise will amount to the aggregate business unit contribution minus the costs of the shared service.

Figure 5.1 shows how this is reflected in accounting statements.

	TOTAL BUSINESS	SALES FORCE	FACTORY	PRODUCT
SALES				
DIRECT COSTS	—	—	—	—
PRODUCT CONTRIBUTION				=====
SHARED FACTORY COSTS	—	—	—	
FACTORY CONTRIBUTION			=====	
SHARED SELLING COSTS	—	—		
BUSINESS UNIT CONTRIBUTION		=====		
SHARED DISTRIBUTION COSTS	—			
PROFIT	=====			

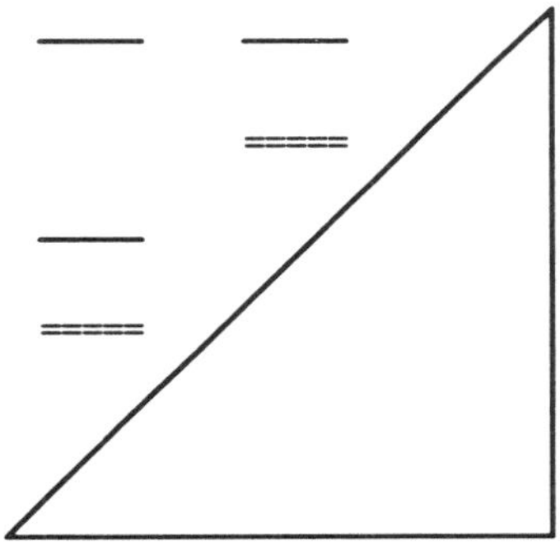

Figure 5.1 The Bermuda Triangle

The bottom right-hand corner is called 'The Bermuda Triangle' because of the number of accountants who have disappeared there after being sent to identify 'the true bottom line profit' of a particular product, factory or business unit. Such exercises always generate more heat than light, ie people pay more attention to the fairness of the apportionments than to the figures under their own control. Rightly or wrongly, fairness does not carry much weight in economics.

The 'direct' approach, however, is not suitable for strategic decisions, eg deciding on the extent of the product range. The least profitable products will defend their place in the scheme of things by reference to the most fixed costs ('You would not save anything if we weren't here') but the most fixed costs will simultaneously defend themselves by reference to the least profitable product (the economies of scale which can be gained).

The evidence for the latter resembles a breakeven chart, as shown in Figure 5.2. The attraction of subcontracting distribution, for example, would be that the cost/volume line (AB) would start from zero: no volume, no cost. The drawback, however, is that the cost/volume line is relatively steep. Conversely, the drawback of an in-house distribution facility is that there is an irreducible level of cost, the attraction being that the line (CD) is relatively shallow. Beyond a certain point (E), it will be asserted, the case for an in-house facility is clear.

Experience suggests, however, that charts based on straight lines, such as in Figure 5.2, and concepts of fixed (or even fixed-per-unit) costs are characteristic of the thinking which underpins the accounting model. Financial management, on the other hand, is more likely to be concerned with curves (the expressions for which are likely to be algebraic rather than arithmetic). We saw the applicability of the diminishing returns curve to volume inducing outlays in the last chapter. They are equally relevant in the context of volume anticipative ones.

INCREMENTALISM

Think what would happen if some other enterprise expresses interest in acquiring part of your business, defined in terms of product, factory or business unit. How would you arrive at a

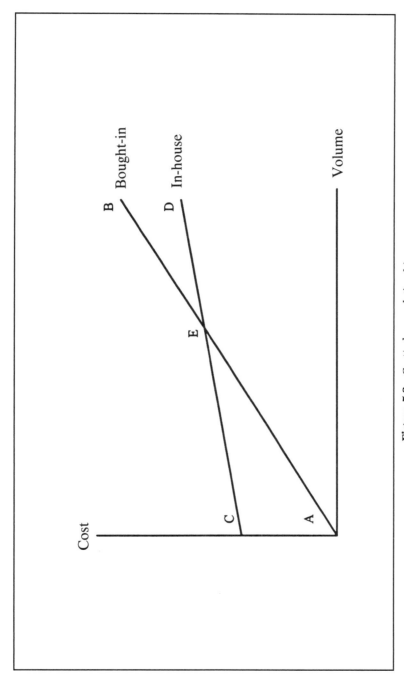

Figure 5.2 Cost/volume relationship

Table 5.1 Incremental analysis I

	Total	Mainline	Secondary
Volume %	100	50	50
£000 Increasing with inflation			
Closing assets	10,500	6,300	4,200
Contribution	4,365	3,365	1,000
(Expansion)	(500)	(300)	(200)
Direct cash flow	3,865	3,065	800
Shared costs	2,000		
Net cash flow	1,865		
Net present value			
(Real cost of capital 10%)	18,650		

price at which it would make sense to sell? Table 5.1 provides a numerical example of this, in the form of an elaboration of strategy A in Chapter 4. There, we put a value of £18.650 million on the total enterprise, based on a cash flow of £1.865 million per annum, increasing with inflation, and a real cost of capital of 10 per cent per annum.

If the enterprise consists of two business units—called Mainline and Secondary, equal in all respects as to size—and the direct cash flows are £3.065 million and £0.800 million respectively, how can we value, say, Secondary? The logic of marginal costing would be to apply the usual multiple to the direct cash flow, ie to say that any price (net of exit costs) over £8.000 million would justify disposal. The logic of absorption costing, on the other hand, would say that half, ie £1.000 million, of the costs of shared services are fairly apportionable to Secondary—hence its net cash flow is minus £0.200 million and we could justify paying anything up to £2.000 million to have the business taken away! It would be difficult to sustain either argument, but what is the alternative?

What you might do is go back to the cost/volume relationship in Figure 5.2 and note that—while the logic is valid within the confines of a short time frame, eg one year—the long-run relationship is given by the line AED. By the time you have recognized economies of scale and combined the slightly different lines of physical distribution, invoicing, etc, you will have something approaching a curve. It is always useful to have some general purpose curves available for when managers do not have an established view, and it will be found that a good starting point is provided by the expression:

$$y = 2x - x^2$$

This is illustrated in Figure 5.3 and is consistent with conditions in which, for example:

☐ a 20 per cent reduction in volume induces only a (20 per cent of 20 per cent =) 4 per cent reduction in cost. In the case we are examining, this perhaps means that dropping one of Secondary's factories would not destroy the case for an in-house distribution system, but neither would it save much: the same number of vehicles would be required to deliver to the same number of customers;

☐ a 50 per cent reduction in volume, however, induces a (50 per cent of 50 per cent =) 25 per cent reduction in cost. At this level, subcontracting becomes more attractive although, of course, the reduction in cost will not match the reduction in volume.

On this basis, Mainline on its own would not be able to justify an in-house distribution system and would pay £1.500 million a year to a third party. This means its cash flow would amount to £1.565 million per annum, increasing with inflation, which, on the usual assumptions, would have a value of £15.650 million. Adding on the Secondary business increases direct cash flow by £0.800 million but increases the costs of distribution, etc, by £0.500 million. Hence the incremental cash flow of Secondary is a net £0.300 million and its value £3.000 million. Therefore, any price in excess of £3.000 million (net of exit costs) would justify selling Secondary and closing the in-house distribution facility. Table 5.2 illustrates this analysis.

Say, for instance, the acquirer was prepared to pay a sum which exceeded exit costs by £3.500 million. Going ahead on this basis would increase the (net present) value of the total enterprise to £19.150 million, although it would lower profits in the current year as a result of the write-off (selling 'assets' carried on the balance sheet at £4.2 million for less than that).

At this stage, however, it is worth noting that you rarely know where strategic evaluations of this kind are going to end.

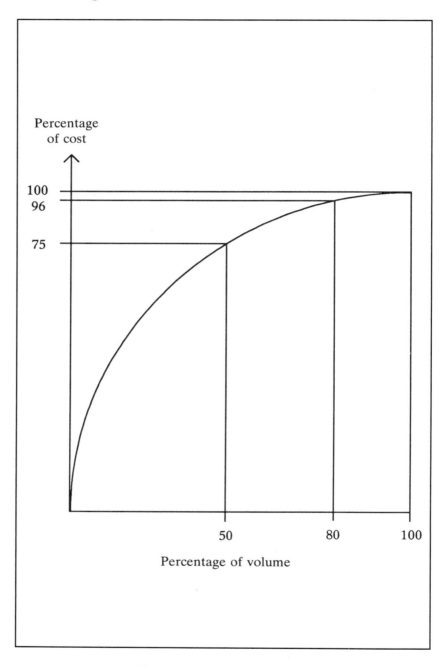

Figure 5.3   Long-run cost curve

Table 5.2 Incremental analysis II

	Total	Mainline	Secondary
Volume %	100	50	50
£000 Increasing with inflation			
Closing assets	10,500	6,300	4,200
Contribution	4,365	3,365	1,000
(Expansion)	(500)	(300)	(200)
Direct cash flow	3,865	3,065	800
Shared costs	2,000	1,500	500
Net cash flow	1,865	1,565	300
Net present value			
(Real cost of capital 10%)	18,650	15,650	3,000

The distribution manager in our example might be prompted to point out that (using the numbers in the example):

☐ the value (= cost of the next best alternative) of the service provided to Mainline is, as we have seen, £1.500 million per annum;

☐ the same service is being provided to Secondary which, on its own, would also have to pay £1.500 million per annum;

☐ so, distribution is providing a service worth in total, on an opportunity cost basis, £3.000 million, compared with its cost of only £2.000 million. Looked at in this way, it is adding value to the extent of £1.000 million per annum which, on the usual assumptions, implies a value of £10.000 million.

Two things develop from this. One is the idea of value centres. If you want to review the place of a shared service in your organization, don't think you can do it by comparing cost with budget or this year with last. The relevant question is simply whether the service is worth more or less than it costs. If it is, perhaps you should steer clear of words with negative connotations like overheads and cost centres, and go instead for value centres.

The second is the recognition that distribution, etc, is a business in its own right. The £3.000 million incremental

Table 5.3 Interpretation of value

		£000
Mainline		15,650
Distribution	10,000	
Secondary	(7,000)	
		3,000
Total		18,650

value of Secondary is seen as the value of the shared services (£10.000 million) minus the stand-alone value of Secondary, which amounts to 10 times its direct cash flow of £0.800 million minus the £1.500 million it would have to pay to get its goods distributed, ie minus £7.000 million. Table 5.3 illustrates this.

Anyone seeing this would be prompted to ask: 'Does selling Secondary necessarily mean closing distribution, or could we replace Secondary with something which has a positive stand-alone value?' The organization could afford to pay quite a premium for a business which met those criteria—and (in a real life case like this) it did. But that is another (corporate strategy) story.

OPTIMIZATION

Deciding on the appropriate level of volume anticipative outlay boils down, in most situations, to a trade-off, eg what degree of flexibility is justifiable in terms of the reduced volume responsive costs? The input to such decisions will take the form of forecast relationships: what is the consequence for volume responsive outlays, per unit, of the various feasible levels of volume anticipative outlays? These will also display diminishing returns: repeated doses of increased volume anticipative costs are likely to induce smaller and smaller reductions in volume responsive outlays, as indicated in Figure 5.4.

First of all, let us look at how we evaluate a reduction in volume responsive costs. This will depend, obviously, on the level of volume, which in turn depends on price, which is a

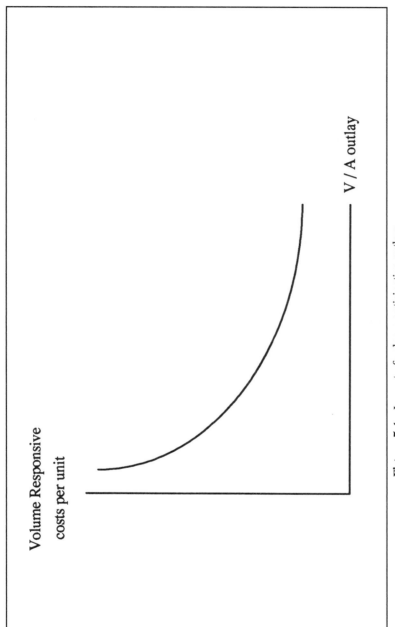

Figure 5.4 Impact of volume anticipative outlays

function of volume responsive costs. Returning to the example developed in Chapter 4, what would be the consequences of reducing volume responsive outlays by 10 per cent, from £2,000 per unit to £1,800? Rerunning the algebra:

Price	$= x$
Volume	$= 22,000 - 4.4x$
Unit contribution now	$= £(x - 1,800)$
Aggregate contribution now	$= £29,920x - 4.4x^2 - 39.6$ million
Maximized where 8.8x	$= 29,920$
Optimum price, therefore, now	$= £3,400$
Volume at that price	$= 7,040$
Unit contribution now	$= £1,600$
Aggregate contribution now	$= £11.264$ million
Present value thereof	$= £17.882$ million
Pv of volume inducing outlay	$= £2.425$ million
Net present value	$= £15.457$ million

That is an improvement of £2.165 million over our previous evaluation. In other words, this reduction would be worth going for if the present value of the increase in volume anticipative costs is less than that.

Armed with this understanding, we can now ask the appropriate production manager what is likely to happen to volume responsive outlays per unit at different levels of volume anticipative outlays. Let us imagine that the £2,000 per unit figure was derived from this year's budget, and assumed that the volume anticipative outlays would amount to £3.250 million. This means that factory contribution, before deducting the costs of volume inducing activities, was budgeted to be £9.000 million − £3.250 million = £5.750 million. Adding in the effect of the increase in volume inducing outlays increases those figures to £9.900 million − £3.250 million, ie to £6.650 million.

As shown in Table 5.4, say it is believed that:

1   The minimum practicable level of volume anticipative outlays is £3.125 million, at which level the volume responsive outlays would be £2,100 per unit. This would suggest a price of £3,550 and volume of 6,380 for a gross contribution of £9.250 million and a factory contribution of £6.125 million.

Table 5.4 Optimizing volume anticipative outlays

	£000				
£000					
Vol. anticipative outlay	3,125	3,250	3,500	4,000	5,000
£ per unit					
Vol. responsive cost	2,100	2,000	1,900	1,800	1,700
Optimum selling price	3,550	3,500	3,450	3,400	3,350
Volume — units	6,380	6,600	6,820	7,040	7,260
£000					
Gross contribution	9,250	9,900	10,571	11,264	11,979
Factory contribution	6,125	6,650	7,071	7,264	6,979

2   Increasing the volume anticipative outlays to £3.500 million would reduce volume responsive outlays to £1,900 per unit, at which level the appropriate price would be £3,450 per unit, for a volume of 6,820, a gross contribution of £10.571 million and a factory contribution, therefore, of £7.071 million.

3   Increasing the volume anticipative outlays to £4.000 million would reduce volume responsive outlays to £1,800 per unit, at which level—as we saw above—the appropriate price would be £3,400 per unit, for a volume of 7,040, a gross contribution of £11.264 million and a factory contribution, therefore, of £7.264 million.

4   Increasing the volume anticipative outlays to £5.000 million would reduce volume responsive outlays to £1,700 per unit, at which level the appropriate price would be £3,350 per unit, for a volume of 7,260, a gross contribution of £11.979 million but a factory contribution, therefore, of only £6.979 million.

On this basis, the level of volume anticipative outlays which maximizes factory contribution is £4.000 million. This would produce a factory contribution of £7.264 million, which—assuming for simplicity that the inertia associated with volume anticipative outlays is also 50 per cent—has a present value of £11.532 million. After deducting the £2.425 million present value of the volume inducing outlays, this means a net present value of £9.107 million.

FORECAST OUTCOME

As usual, after we have made our decision—in this case on the level of volume anticipative outlays—we can log the expected outcome in terms of cash flows, discounted at the cost of capital. This is summarized in Table 5.5.

Table 5.5 Forecast outcome

Year	Factor	£000 Absolute	Discounted
1	0.866	4,464	3,866
2	0.750	3,814	2,859
3	0.649	2,002	1,300
4	0.561	1,051	591
etc	etc	etc	269
			122
			56
			25
			11
			5
			2
			1
			9,107

We can also, as usual, articulate the numbers by means of the benchmarking process:

	£000
Opening net present value	9,107
Cost of capital	1,412
Cash (generation)	(4,064)
Benchmark	6,055

For reassurance, this can be checked, as shown in Table 5.6.

Thus far, we have kept the assumed inertia in the business at a constant 50 per cent. In the next chapter, we look at how this might be improved.

Table 5.6 A year later

Year	Factor	£000 Absolute	£000 Discounted
1	0.866	3,814	3,303
2	0.750	2,002	1,501
3	0.649	1,051	683
etc	etc	etc	310
			141
			64
			29
			13
			6
			3
			1
			1
			6,055

6

Volume Sustaining Outlays

In this chapter, we look at those outlays which are incurred with a view to enhancing the probability that customers will be satisfied and come back for more. The total quality movement has drawn attention to the importance of being close to the customer but the control of selling costs is something of a dark continent. In this chapter, we see how the evaluation, optimization and evaluation approach described earlier can be applied to these outlays.

FINANCIAL MANAGEMENT OF QUALITY

In evaluating the forecast outcome of our pricing and volume inducing decisions, we made the assumption that the inertia applicable to the business in question was 50 per cent, ie that for every unit of volume achieved this year there was a 50 per cent chance of a repeat next year. This inertia is very important: it is far cheaper to keep a satisfied customer than to find a new one—or convert a dissatisfied one. We now turn to the influences on this inertia and ways of improving it.

In part, this has a direct relationship with quality. Advertising may persuade a customer to try your product but, if the quality is inadequate, it is unlikely that the customer will come back for more. The obverse is also likely to be true: investing in quality, but not communicating it to potential customers, is unlikely to be a viable strategy.

The total quality management philosophy has been very popular in recent years. Under various acronyms it has been adapted to form the basis for a complete overhaul of the operations of a business across a broad range of industries.

However, very few organizations have not run into serious obstacles in the shape of conflicts with established control systems. 'What course of action should I follow?' asks the manager. 'That which is implied by our commitment to quality or that which has the most favourable effect on my performance indicators (and, consequently, on my earnings)?'

Some examples of these conflicts are as follows:

☐ *Operational.* The consultant says a patient can go home but the sister says not because 'I have no one to take his place until next week and I shall therefore fall short of the bed occupancy target against which my performance is measured.'

The problem here is that performance measurement has been seen as a means to performance improvement —which may or (as in this example) may not be the case. In addition, the 'attention-directing' attributes of the information have been suppressed, eg the question of whether scheduling techniques could be improved.

The solution is to reposition performance measurement as a subset of progress monitoring, eg prompting the question of whether future potential has been forgone in order to achieve measured results.

☐ *Tactical.* The sales manager says that a customer can be expected to give more business only if the product is modified to the customer's specification. The production manager refuses to do so on the grounds that stopping and starting the line will increase set-up costs and scrap. This will have an adverse effect on the comparison of average costs with budget, which forms the basis of his performance measurement.

The problem here is that the yardsticks against which performance is measured are inappropriate given the actual conditions. No attempt has been made to assess whether the business overall would show better or worse results if the opportunity were to be pursued.

The solution is to restrict the use of average costs to accounting tasks such as stock valuation, preparing specific job costs in order to assess profitability and measure performance. Consideration should be given to accumulating these job costs into customer profitability reports.

☐ *Strategic*. The development manager reports that the shelf-life for the new product is not yet up to market needs and the launch planned for next quarter should be postponed. The general manager overrides this on the grounds that postponement would have an adverse effect on profits and on earnings per share, which is the basis on which his performance is measured and on which he is rewarded.

The problem here is that backward-looking accounting information is being used as though it provided decision support.

The solution requires accounting numbers to be positioned as stewardship/monitoring information and a distinctive financial management approach to be developed. In particular, alternatives should be evaluated in terms of their impact on the value of the business (its cash generating potential).

Underpinning much of this thinking is the fact that, while the costs of rectification and failure can be measured, the value of prevention cannot—because it is based on subjective judgements. Beware of those who advocate that all will be well if you combine some non-financial measures with your financial ones (the balanced scorecard and all that). The real difference is between that which can be measured (because it has already happened) and that which can only be assessed (because it has not happened yet). The future is characterized by uncertainty; managing that uncertainty (by synthesising judgements into decisions) rather than seeking to find the 'truth' is one of the features which distinguishes players from spectators.

The task of reorienting management information along the lines suggested is not easy, but if you are able to achieve it you will have a financial management structure suited to quality management. In other words, you can boast financial management of quality.

THE LONG AND THE SHORT OF IT

In some cases, the trade-off inherent in the quality arena is between volume responsive costs and inertia. In other words,

Table 6.1 Evaluating lower quality

Year	Factor	£000 Absolute	£000 Discounted
1	0.866	5,179	4,485
2	0.750	3,351	2,513
3	0.649	1,407	914
4	0.561	591	333
etc	etc	etc	127
			48
			19
			7
			3
			1
			8,450

the variable cost of a product can be reduced (eg by lowering the quality of the materials specified) with no initial impact on volume (because customers are expecting it to be the same as previous offerings) but a significant reduction in the number who come back for more (because they have been disappointed).

To see how this might be viewed, let us return to our running example at the point reached in Table 5.4. Specifically, let us imagine that the company could reduce its volume responsive costs from £1,800 to £1,700 per unit by downgrading its specifications. As we saw, this would move the optimum price down to £3,350 per unit and increase volume to 7,260, which would yield a gross contribution of £11.979 million. Net of volume anticipative costs of £4.000 million, this means a contribution (before deducting volume inducing outlays of £2.800 million) of £7.979 million. But if the resulting dissatisfaction among customers brought the inertia down to 40 per cent, the value of the business would be reduced from the £9.107 million we saw in Table 5.5 to £8.450 million, as shown in Table 6.1.

Note that this assumes that the inertia of the volume anticipative outlays could be forced down accordingly. If this were not the case, the impact would be even more damaging. The most important point is that in this example—as in many instances in practice—the choice boils down to a conflict between short-run profits (which would be improved in this case) and the long-run value of the business (which would be weakened). In the present context, we shall assume that the latter prevails, ie the company chooses not to reduce the quality of its product.

THE CUSTOMER DIMENSION

Attention to quality has reinforced another trend, namely that towards looking at financial numbers of all kinds in a customer context. Understanding the relative profitability of trade with different market sectors such as:

☐ retail as distinct from wholesale;

☐ original equipment as distinct from replacement;

☐ domestic as distinct from export;

and as between customers within those sectors is at least as important in many organizations as understanding the profitability of different products. Indeed, it may well be worth losing money on some products within the trade with a customer whose business overall is valuable.

Product profitability analyses fit very well with traditional financial and hence integrated accounts, not least because of the natural affinity with the product costs which are used for stock valuations. It is important to recognize, however, that customer profitability analysis does not. In particular, notice how costs which are direct in the product dimension (eg advertising) can be indirect in the customer dimension; conversely, costs which are indirect in the product dimension (eg selling and distribution) can be direct in the customer dimension.

For this reason, customer profitability analyses are usually operated alongside the traditional management accounts rather than within them. The information customer profitability analysis provide complements, rather than replaces, that provided by product profitability analyses. As a result, they may provide a better testing ground for techniques such as activity based costing.

Reporting customer and product profitability calls for a well-designed format, a generic version of which is illustrated

Table 6.2 Matrix of accountability

£000	Product A	B	Shared costs of selling	Combined
Contribution				
Market x	1,000	700	(300)	1,400
Market y	300	200	(200)	300
Total	1,300	900	(500)	1,700
Shared costs of production	(250)	(150)		(400)
Combined	1,050	750	(500)	1,300
Administration costs				(300)
Profit				1,000

in Table 6.2. Those interested in a particular product can look down the appropriate column, while those interested in a particular market can look across the appropriate row. The finance function needs to be able to look both ways at once.

MANAGEMENT'S DARK CONTINENT

Another important element in getting satisfied customers to come back for more is the company's sales force. In more stable times, this function tended to be seen as very much an operational-level activity. Targets were set and performance measured in very simple terms, such as the number of boxes sold in a given period.

As the rate of change increased, key tactical issues came to the surface. Prices are no longer set once a year at budget time by top management as part of the budgeting exercise. Flexibility is the keyword and sales managers have to have authority to negotiate deals in the light not only of customer needs but also competitive activity.

This has created a need for development programmes in many businesses so that sales executives can be introduced to the terminology of finance, the dynamics of the business in question and any particular limiting factors such as capacity constraints. Special attention needs to be paid to the implications of volume changes on current assets such as stocks and debtors.

Predictably, recent years have seen the sales force recognized as a key player at the strategic level of management. No function is closer to the customer or more aware of competitive activity than the sales force. As these are the starting points for the formulation of strategy, a further phase of development is required—top sales people need to understand concepts such as cash flow, the cost of capital, and hence net present values.

But how much to invest in selling activity? Last year's actual plus inflation, or some arbitrary percentage of budgeted sales, are common, but not praiseworthy. In fact, they may be counter-productive and overlook the vital question which springs from the logic of strategic financial management: what is the *value* of the sales force?

In terms of economy and efficiency, it might be worth comparing the costs of a sales force with some third-party alternative, eg agents on commission. In terms of effectiveness, however, it is necessary to ask the question 'What benefits arise as a result of having a sales force?' One benefit might be of a volume inducing nature. For example, where the practice is for customers to place orders with the sales representative, it moves the demand curve to the right—the greater the investment, the greater the volume of sales at any given price level. Diminishing returns are to be expected, and the evaluation and monitoring procedures will be like those we saw for advertising in Chapter 4.

Additionally, however, it is likely that the attention of the sales force—identifying specific needs and problems—is in the nature of a volume sustaining activity. The greater that attention, the more likely the customer is to be satisfied and come back for more. Quantifying this may be more difficult, however, because of the relative newness of the topic as far as sales managers are concerned.

In some instances, it might be useful to ask stark questions like 'What do you think would be the consequence of halving/ doubling our investment?' The message must be communicated that this is not an area where the accountant has objectively verifiable knowledge or a claim to superior foresight. What is required in the first instance is the local expert's subjective judgement as to the relationship between the investment in volume sustaining activities and the resulting inertia, a generic version of which appears as Figure 6.1.

EVALUATIONS

Let us see how an increase in inertia is evaluated. Table 6.3 shows how, in the now familiar layout, an improvement from 50 to 55 per cent would enhance the value of the business as it stood in Table 5.5 by £1.043 million to £10.150 million.

This provides the basis for choosing between the alternatives open to the business. Table 6.4 shows how this might look if it is believed that:

1   The minimum practicable level of investment in volume sustaining activities is £1.200 million, at which level the profit would be £3.264 million but inertia would be 45 per cent, producing a gross present value of £8.217 million. Deducting the present value of the outlay (£1.758 million on the usual assumptions but assuming the lower inertia also applies to the outlay) from the gross figure produces a net figure of £6.459 million.

2   The budgeted investment was £1.400 million, at which level the profit would be £3.064 million and the inertia the 50 per cent used in the worked examples thus far. Deducting the net present value of the outlay (£2.223 million on the usual assumptions) from the £9.107 million shown in the fourth column of Table 6.3 produces a final figure of £6.884 million.

3   Increasing the investment to £1.800 million would reduce the profit to £2.664 million but improve the inertia to 55 per cent, producing the expectations shown in the sixth column of Table 6.3. Deducting the net present value of the outlay (£3.115 million on the usual assumption, but assuming the higher inertia figure applies to the outlay) from the £10.150 million shown in Table 6.3 produces a final figure of £7.035 million.

4   Increasing the investment to £2.600 million would reduce the profit to £1.864 million but improve the inertia to 60

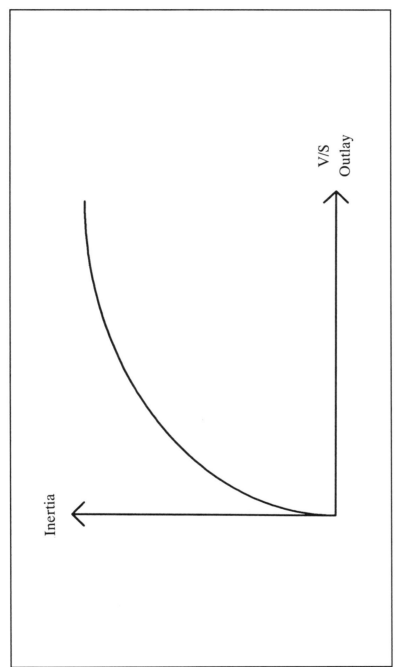

Figure 6.1   Impact of volume sustaining outlays

per cent, producing a gross present value of £11.413. Deducting the net present value of the outlay (£4.952 million on the usual assumption, but assuming the higher inertia figure applies to the outlay) produces a final figure of £6.461 million.

Table 6.3 Evaluating a 10% improvement in inertia

| Year | Discount factor | Cash flows £000 | | | |
| | | 50% Inertia | | 55% Inertia | |
		Absolute	Discounted	Absolute	Discounted
1	0.866	4,464	3,866	4,464	3,866
2	0.750	3,814	2,859	4,195	3,146
3	0.649	2,002	1,300	2,423	1,572
4	0.561	1,051	591	1,399	784
etc	etc	etc	269	etc	393
			122		196
			56		98
			25		49
			11		24
			5		12
			2		6
			1		3
					1
			9,107		10,150

Table 6.4 Optimizing volume sustaining outlays

| Inertia | £000 V/S outlays | £000 Present values | | |
		Contrib'n	V/S	Net
45%	1,200	8,217	1,758	6,459
50%	1,400	9,107	2,223	6,884
55%	1,800	10,150	3,115	7,035
60%	2,600	11,413	4,952	6,461

On this basis, the forecast outcome is as in the sixth column of Table 6.3, and we can establish a benchmark for next year, as follows:

	£000
Opening net present value	7,035
Cost of capital 15.5%	1,090
Cash flow	(2,664)
Benchmark	5,461

This can be checked by rerunning the figures one year on, as shown in Table 6.5

Table 6.5   One year on

| | | Cash flows £000 | |
| | Discount | 55% Inertia | |
Year	factor	Absolute	Discounted
2	0.866	3,156	2,733
3	0.750	1,822	1,366
4	0.649	1,052	683
etc	etc	etc	341
			170
			85
			42
			21
			11
			5
			3
			1
			5,461

Now that we have covered the main items affecting hope and its conversion into expectations, we can turn to those affecting faith and its conversion into hope.

Regenerative Outlays

In this chapter, we bring together the evaluations
from the previous four, to show the consolidated
'hope' and 'expectations' components of the value of
the business. In particular, we see how a modifica-
tion of the budgeting process enables strategy and
tactics to be firmly linked. Finally, the 'faith' element
of value is incorporated, to bring us back to the total
business value introduced in Chapter 2.

THE MINIMALIST OPTION

At the end of the last chapter, we had reached the point where
the value of the chosen strategies amounted to £7.035 million.
The way in which this had been built up means that it
represents both expectations (outcome of decisions already
made) and hope (outcome of decisions currently being made).
To subdivide the figure into its two components, we need to go
back to the minimum practical outlays in each case. These
were:

☐ no investment in advertising, the resulting elasticity being
summed up in an expression $y = 18,000 - 3.6x$;

☐ a £3.125 million investment in volume anticipative outlays,
at which level the volume responsive costs would have
been £2,100 per unit. The optimum price would have been
£3,550 per unit, which would result in a volume of 5,220
units, a gross contribution of £7.569 million and hence a
factory contribution of £4.444 million;

☐ a £1.200 million investment in volume sustaining activities, at which level the inertia would be 45 per cent, resulting in a profit of £3.244 million and a net present value of £4.753 million, as shown in Table 7.1.

Table 7.1 The minimalist option

| | | £000 | |
Year	Factor	Absolute	Discounted
1	0.866	3,244	2,809
2	0.750	1,533	1,150
3	0.649	724	470
4	0.561	342	192
etc	etc	etc	79
			32
			13
			5
			2
			1
			4,753

We then advanced beyond that, in the following order:

☐ Investing £2.800 million (present value £2.425 million) in volume inducing activities, which moved the demand curve to $y = 22,000 - 4.4x$. On its own, ie on unchanged volume responsive costs, this would have meant that the volume would have been 6,380 and gross contribution £9.251 million. Net of the volume anticipative and sustaining outlays, this would come down to £4.926 million, which has a present value (still assuming 45 per cent inertia) of £7.217 million, or £4.792 million net of the outlay. From this angle, the volume inducing outlays have increased the value of the business by £0.039 million.

☐ Increasing the investment in volume anticipative costs to £4.000 million brought the volume anticipative costs down to £1,800 per unit and the optimum price to £3,400 per unit. This meant an increase in volume to 7,040 units and in contribution to £11.264 million, ie £2.013 million above the figure in the previous paragraph, or £1.138 million after deducting the increased outlay. The present value of this (still assuming 45 per cent inertia) is £1.667 million.

☐ Had we stopped at this point, the net present value of the projected cash flows of the business would have been £1.706 million above the minimalist case at £6.459 million, as shown in the top line of Table 6.4.

☐ Finally, as we saw in the third line of Table 6.4, increasing the volume sustaining outlays to £1.800 million had the effect of improving inertia to 55 per cent and the net present value to £7.035 million.

It might therefore be argued that it would be fair to summarize the value of the business as:

	£000	
Expectations—the minimalist option		4,753
Hope		
Volume inducing outlays	39	
Volume anticipative	1,667	
Volume sustaining	576	
		2,282
Combined		7,035

Be careful! This is the sort of additive logic which fits well with the accounting model but not the financial management model. It reflects the thinking illustrated in the top half of Figure 7.1.

To see how restrictive this is, let us evaluate what would happen if volume anticipative and sustaining outlays were optimized as above, but the volume inducing outlays were not undertaken.

The demand curve would fall back to $y = 18,000 - 3.6x$ and the optimization decision would flow thus:

Unit contribution	$= £(x - 1,800)$
Aggregate contribution	$= £(24,480x - 3.6x^2 - 32,400)$
Maximized where	$7.2x = 24,480$
ie optimum price	$= 3,400$ as before
but volume only	$= 5,760$
and aggregate contribution	$= £9.216$ million

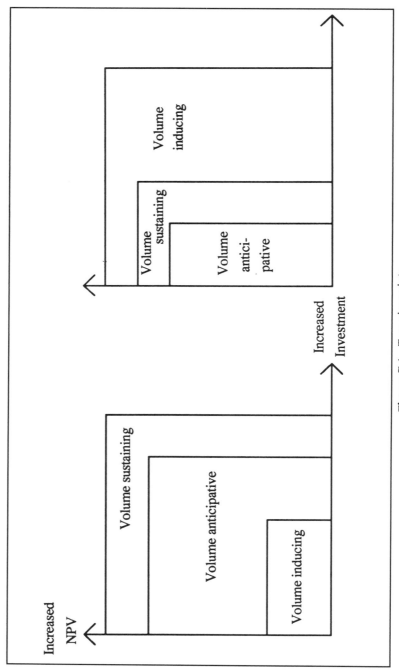

Figure 7.1 Two viewpoints

Net of the volume anticipative and sustaining outlays this comes down to £3.416 million, the present value of which, assuming 55 per cent inertia is £5.911 million. From this angle, the value of the volume inducing outlays is £7.035 million — £5.911 million, ie £1.124 million. If the volume sustaining outlays were then reset at the minimalist £1.200 million figure, the net present value of the business would fall back only £28,000, leaving a value of £1.130 million attributable to the volume anticipative outlays. The bottom half of Figure 7.1 refers.

In the same way, if the volume anticipative outlays were reset at the original £3.125 million and there were no volume inducing outlays, it can be shown that the value of the business would be £4.575 million, ie on its own the increase in the volume sustaining outlays would have *lowered* the value of the business by £0.178 million. Rather as in analysing cost variances, the answers depend on the order in which the questions are asked. At this strategic level, however, the impact of the interaction is much greater, as we have seen.

Perhaps the most important lesson here is to be aware of the dangers of evaluating dimensions of strategy in isolation. On their own, the values of the three investments we have looked at would appear to be worth:

	£000
Volume inducing	39
Volume anticipative	1,130
Volume sustaining	(178)
Subtotal	991
But there is an interaction worth	1,291
Bringing their combined value to	2,282

STRATEGIC BUDGETING

This is perhaps the point at which to recognize some of the obstacles to thinking and acting long term. Privately-owned businesses do not have so much difficulty (except when they need to persuade bankers to increase lending) as publicly-quoted ones, where directorial security is undoubtedly dependent on share price and the latter is arguably a function of reported profits—or, at least, short-term forecasts of profits.

Be on the look-out for linguistic problems. In particular, having stressed the need to think long term, don't be surprised if you are quoted as having said that the short term does not matter. Of course it does—the long term is a series of short terms which need to be negotiated. You may have to raise the question 'When does the long term start?' It is not a matter of saying that the end of year 2 is, of itself, more important than the end of year 1. It is a matter of saying that from here to the end of year 2 is more important than from here to the end of year 1: the former embraces the latter.

The question, therefore, is never one of *whether or not* a benefit is expected to arise as a result of a particular outlay; it is always one of *whether enough* benefit is expected to arise in view of the length of the interval between outlay and benefit. What constitutes *enough* in this context is, of course, a function of the value of time, otherwise known as the cost of capital.

This leads naturally to a consideration of the question of how long-term strategic evaluations are linked to short-term tactical controls, such as budgets. All too often the process regresses, in the sense that the budget is described as the first year of the plan. The net effect is to import all the gamesmanship associated with budgets to the strategic level. You know the sequence:

☐ The division presents a budget or plan showing, say, a 20 per cent return on investment.

☐ The parent company asks 'Can't you make it 22 per cent?'

☐ The division says 'Yes, but we would have to defer or cancel some long-term investment' and the growth rate will fall back from, say, 8 per cent per annum to 5 per cent per annum.

Apart from teasing out the contingencies built in by the division (who know that the parent will ask for more), the only decision being made here is where on the growth versus return line to be. How a 20 per cent return growing at 8 per cent per annum compares with a 22 per cent return growing at 5 per cent per annum is a matter of calculation, the key input being the cost of capital.

An alternative is to express the budget in a way which reflects the strategic decisions and expectations, and therefore provides a basis on which to monitor their implementation. Reverting to our worked example, notice how, in total, we changed the situation, as between the minimalist option and our preferred pattern of outlays:

☐ profit has been reduced from £3.244 million to £2.664 million;

☐ net present value has been increased from £4.753 million to £7.035 million.

In other words, our decisions to invest in additional volume inducing, anticipative and sustaining outlays have had a £0.580 million adverse effect on profit but a £2.282 million favourable effect on net present value. Expressing the budget in that way, so as to highlight the choices made, can be very helpful. Businesses which have longer-range projections—incorporating faith as well as hope and expectations—will be able to portray the figures as in Figure 7.2.

The message needs to be that tactics follow strategy, not the other way around.

THE OTHER INTANGIBLES

Early in this book, we noted the importance—given the rapid rate of change in the business environment—of investments in intangibles such as research, development, marketing, training and information. Marketing outlays are usually volume inducing and we saw in Chapter 5 how these could be evaluated and monitored. Training usually produces benefits in terms of quality, and information is often vital to knowing what keeps customers satisfied—both of which were alluded to in our consideration of volume sustaining outlays.

We now turn to research and development, which hold the key to innovation both in terms of product and process. In financial management terms, the product benefits move the demand curve up the chart (more volume at the same general

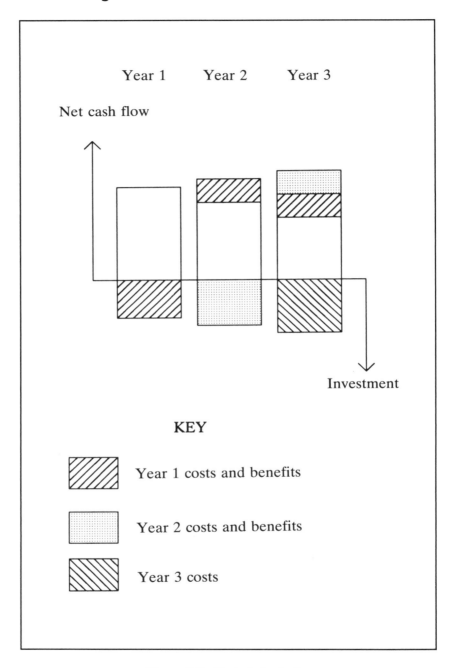

Figure 7.2 Strategic budgeting

price level) and therefore augment volume inducing outlays. The process benefits may offer lower volume responsive costs or may push the cost/volume relationship down the chart —lower volume responsive costs at any given level of volume anticipative outlay. Both may improve the quality of what is offered, with a consequent improvement in inertia.

Investments in research and development involve the most subjective judgements of all and have the longest time frames. Beware of the response 'I can't quantify the benefits, they are judgemental'. In many organizations, the breakthrough for proactive financial management has been getting people to recognize that the words judgemental and quantifiable are not mutually exclusive. It is not a matter of finance second-guessing the technical experts, but of helping to quantify their judgements (drawing on knowledge of other parts of the business) so as to reach a conclusion as to the optimum investment. As usual, diminishing returns are likely to be a feature, so it is a matter of identifying where the cost and benefit lines cross.

It is also important to stress the value of time. As the financial controller of a successful computer manufacturer put it:

> A few years ago, one of my main tasks was to warn researchers if it looked like they were going to overspend their project budgets. Today, I am likely to be warning them of how much we stand to lose if we are late getting the product to market. On a typical project, a 25 per cent overrun is preferable to a month's delay.

Because they are operating at the margin—building on (ie multiplying) the values of the other outlays—these 'regenerative' outlays are likely to show the most spectacular returns. Putting it another way, their successful pursuit will make it feasible to maintain or enhance the levels of volume inducing, anticipative and sustaining outlays which, thus far, we have assumed would fade away (immediately in the first case, in line with the assumed inertia for the other two).

We will now bring our detailed example together: strategy A from the tale of two strategies, later subdivided into Mainstream, Secondary and Distribution. Specifically, let us add to our detailed example an assumption that a regenerative outlay of £0.800 million is consistent with keeping all key figures

Table 7.2 Strategy A

Year	Factor	£000 Absolute	£000 Discounted
1	0.866	1,865	1,615
2	0.750	1,958	1,469
3	0.649	2,056	1,334
4	0.561	2,159	1,213
5	etc	etc	1,103
6			1,002
7			912
8			828
↓			} 9,174
Infinity			
			18,650

(including itself) rising in line with inflation. This would bring us down to a net cash flow this year of £1.865 million and the familiar net present value of £18.650 million, now shown in a year-by-year form in Table 7.2.

This means we now have a three way split of our value:

	£000
Expectations	4,753
Hope	2,282
Faith	11,615
Total	18,650

As experience is gained with this approach, the significance of this split will grow. One chief executive likes to compare the percentages across the businesses which comprise the group in order to have rules of thumb appropriate to their maturity and prospects. These can then guide the discussion, as follows:

☐ The higher the proportion in the faith column, the more rapid the growth which is being projected, nudging the discussion in the direction of innovation and hence research and development.

☐ The higher the proportion in expectations, the more important, as we have seen, will be matters concerning volume inducing, anticipative and sustaining outlays.

☐ The higher the proportion in the expectations column, the more the business will resemble a cash cow, and the emphasis is likely to be on pricing and volume responsive outlays.

It has to be acknowledged that many people are uncomfortable when such a high proportion of value is in the later years—half beyond year 8 for strategy A, which is just keeping up with inflation. Think, however, of the message received from share prices. A dividend yield of around 4 per cent, even if growing, will take very many years to accumulate to the share price. In other words, share prices are a high multiple of current cash flows. Some would argue that this means the stock market—contrary to the blame heaped on it—is actually *long*-termist.

8

Managing Uncertainty

Whereas the accounting model seeks single point precision, the world of the financial manager is characterized by uncertainty. In this chapter, we note the problems inherent in the traditional (academic) approach, ie to suppress consideration of uncertainty by augmenting the cost of capital. Some of the benefits of an alternative approach—incorporating uncertainty within forecast cash flows—are identified, and the links with capital structure explored.

A CONSPIRACY OF SILENCE

The cost of capital (along with cash flow) is a foundation stone of modern financial management. We noted in Chapter 1 that if it is set too high, the company will turn away viable projects and shrink relative to the competition, but if it is set too low, the company will risk insolvency. Yet boards of directors are universally unwilling to go public on what figure they do use—or how they arrived at it.

In recent years, the cost of capital has received considerable attention in the public sector because the Treasury determines what profit an enterprise can make by multiplying the current cost of its assets by a percentage representing the long-run real cost of money. In the newly-privatized sector, the water industry regulator has accused his industry of using too high a cost of capital when making decisions on capital investment and pricing, against the interests of consumers.

You might expect such an important topic to be well covered

in the literature, but you would be disappointed. There are numerous articles and books by accounting academics but, as might be expected, they think in terms of ascertaining what the (objectively verifiable) actual cost was in the past. They usually start with last year's balance sheet, establish a cost for each component (principally equity and borrowings) and calculate a weighted average. The difficult component is equity, of course, because in accounting terms it does not have a cost—it is entitled to what is left after all other stakeholders' legitimate claims have been met.

Again in the interests of objective verifiability, the most popular approach relies on an analysis of past returns on equities, coupled with a hypothesis that the extent of past fluctuations in its small lot share price indicates the risk associated with a particular company's business. For a fee, some academics will calculate your share price's relative volatility and tell you to three places of a percentage point what, hypothetically, your cost of capital has been.

The conventional wisdom is that investors are risk averse, ie the greater the return they will demand, as shown in Figure 8.1. Stated in those terms, the logic is clearly contrived: if investors are in a position to demand a particular return, how can they be said to be at risk? Some numbers might help to clarify the issue, and most adherents of this 'capital asset pricing model' theory like to use the average returns on the American market over the last 60 years.

The average return on American equities over the period 1932–92 was 12 per cent against a 4 per cent risk free rate. Thus, if you believe that investors expect what their ancestors achieved, you will say that, on average, the cost of equity will be eight points above the risk free rate at any point in time. If the risk free rate is the 15.5 per cent we have used throughout this book, the cost of equity capital would be said to be 23.5 per cent on average. On this basis, £123,500 to be received in a year's time has a present value of £100,000. In this way, some scales are put to the risk/reward line, as illustrated in Figure 8.2.

If the price of your company's shares has fluctuated twice as much as the market, the theorists say, add 16 points to the risk free rate, ie call it 31.5 per cent. The same forecast would now be given a present value of only £93,916, which exposes the fallacy on which the model is based. It may be useful, however, to look more deeply into the data.

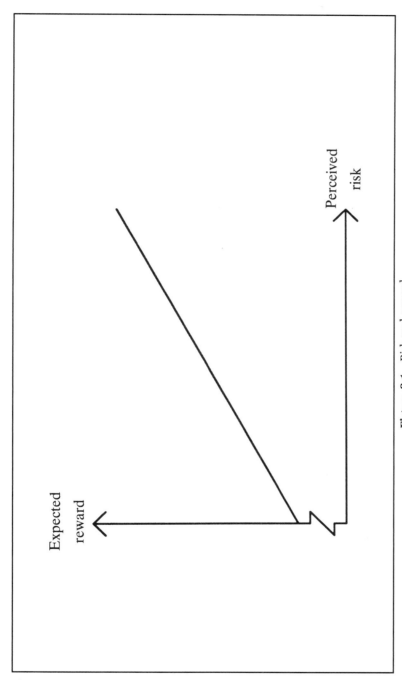

Figure 8.1 Risk and reward

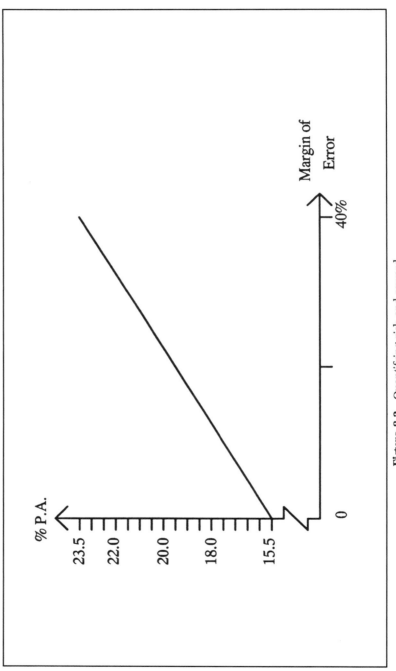

Figure 8.2 Quantifying risk and reward

If you were to do so, you might be surprised by the variation in the annual rate of return: up to plus or minus 40 points from that average of 12 per cent. Statisticians would say that, provided you believe the future will be like the past, you can be 95 per cent confident that the return will be between minus 28 per cent and plus 52 per cent!

If we look at this from the viewpoint of the insider looking out (as opposed to the outsider-looking-in viewpoint of the theorists) we might say that:

☐ For the average equity, £100,000 represents not £123,500 discounted at 23.5 per cent but a range between £83,500 and £163,500 discounted at the risk free rate of 15.5 per cent. In effect, we are distilling that range into a certainty equivalent of £115,500, ie £8,000 below its midpoint (this deduction representing 8 per cent of the value).

☐ For the doubly volatile equity, £100,000 represents not £131,500 discounted at 31.5 per cent but a range between £51,500 and £211,500 discounted at 15.5 per cent. In effect, we are distilling that range into a certainty equivalent of £115,500, ie £16,000 below its midpoint (this deduction representing 16 per cent of the value).

Note that this has not changed the assumed relationship between risk and reward. Deducting an amount from the statistician's expected value has exactly the same effect as using a higher discount rate, as can be seen from Figure 8.3.

But the practical implications are startling. If we position uncertainty alongside cash flow, rather than suppress it within the cost of capital:

☐ We can make sure that it is given adequate attention in the project formulation stage, ie managers must consider and quantify the margin of error in their forecasts (as they are used to doing at the tactical level).

☐ We can dissociate it from the notion that the cost of capital is a single-point, backward-looking concept, ie we can have different pure interest rates (in line with published yield curves) and different margins of error (as input by managers) for different time frames.

☐ We can also dissociate it from the academics' obsession

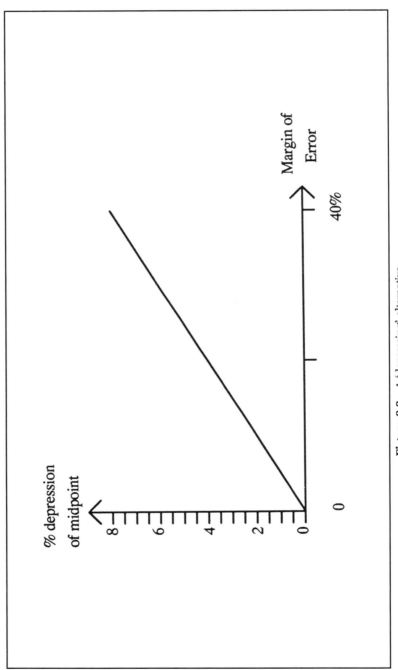

Figure 8.3 A 'depressing' alternative

with fluctuations in small lot share prices. Projects within privately-owned businesses and in the public sector are also subject to margins of error, and from society's point of view carry a commensurate risk, which should be allowed for.

☐ We can assemble projects into strategies and use the evaluations as the starting point for monitoring progress in their implementation.

We don't have to depress the expected value by one-fifth of the margin of error as in the above examples. We can substitute a relationship derived from our current financial position, notably the margin of error in our overall cash flow projections, our capital structure, etc.

Just as the net present value approach to discounting cash flows has ousted the internal rate of return approach which used to be seen as a contender, the odds are that associating uncertainty with projected cash flows rather than the cost of capital will become the norm in financial management.

AGGREGATION

To see how this affects strategic decisions, let us take a simple example of a volume anticipative outlay which is to be treated as capital expenditure in the accounting model. A very high proportion of businesses use a discounted cash flow approach in such cases—at least to sell a project to higher levels of management if not as a decision-support tool.

Those preparing the proposal should be encouraged to recognize the margin of error in their projections. Say Project 1 requires an investment of £1 million, to be paid in 12 months' time. Rather than saying that it is expected to bring savings of, say, £400,000 per annum increasing in line with inflation of 5 per cent per annum in each of the subsequent five years, it would be more realistic to say that these savings are subject to an increasing margin of error as the time frame extends. Table 8.1 shows how this would be evaluated, on the assumption of a 5:1 risk reward ratio and margins of error which increase steadily from +/− 20 per cent to +/− 100 per cent.

Table 8.1 Project 1

Evaluation of savings of £400,000 increasing with inflation

Year	Factor	Percentage error	depression	Cash flows £000 absolute	discounted
1	0.866	–	–	(1,000)	(866)
2	0.750	20	4	384	288
3	0.649	40	8	386	251
4	0.561	60	12	388	218
5	0.486	80	16	389	189
6	0.421	100	20	389	164
					244

Table 8.2 Project 2

Evaluation of savings of £100,000 increasing with inflation

Year	Factor	Percentage error	depression	Cash flows £000 absolute	discounted
1	0.866	–	–	(250)	(216)
2	0.750	20	4	96	72
3	0.649	20	4	101	65
4	0.561	80	16	92	52
5	0.486	80	16	97	47
6	0.421	100	20	96	40
					60

Another project in the same business might require an investment of £250,000 and offer savings the midpoint of the range of possible outcomes of which is £100,000, increasing with inflation over the subsequent five years, but subject to an irregular pattern of margins of error, as shown in Table 8.2. Where uncertainty is allowed for by augmenting the cost of capital, this irregularity is likely to be ignored. Where it is allowed for by depressing the cash flows, it is easily accommodated, as here.

The two net present values can be combined and—because the same cost of capital has been used—the usual benchmarking approach can be applied across the business, as follows:

		£000	
	Project 1	Project 2	Total
Opening net present value	244	60	304
Cost of capital 15.5%	38	9	47
Cash absorption	1,000	250	1,250
Benchmark	1,282	319	1,601

One year on, when the installation phase has been completed, is an ideal time to review the projects in order to see whether the projected cash flows have a present value in line with the benchmark. It may be that market conditions have changed, with the result that volume will be lower than originally projected, or it may be that the equipment is not as productive as was expected. Whatever the reason, comparing what is now projected with what should have been projected had the original forecasts been confirmed provides strategic account-ability and feedback.

THE ETERNAL TRIANGLE

Since its inception, the discounted cash flow technique has been applied—not surprisingly—as a means of linking cash flows and the cost of capital in order to provide values. In the early days, the internal rate of return variant was quite popular. Here the question being asked was 'At what rate do I have to discount the projected cash flows in order to arrive at an answer of zero?' If the solution rate exceeded the cost of capital, the project was classed as viable.

As time has gone by, however, the limitations of this method have been recognized. It is a trial and error approach rather than a straight mathematical task, it can produce more than one answer when cash flows fluctuate, and it ignores differences in the cost of capital and uncertainty over time. In the context of this book, it also fails to provide a starting point for that vital element of control: monitoring.

The net present value variant suffers from none of these deficiencies. Here the task is to ask 'What is the net present value of the projected cash flows, discounted at the cost of capital?' It is a straightforward mathematical task, easily assimilated in spreadsheet models, it produces only one answer and, as shown above, it can cope with different margins of error. It also provides the starting point for strategic monitoring, (and hence accountability and feedback) by means of benchmarking.

What is only just beginning to receive widespread recognition is that the net present value approach can—as it has in previous chapters in this book—be applied not only to projected cash flows but also to future values. When we are calculating the benchmark, we are putting a value on a project (or a dimension of strategy, or a total business) in a year's time. Going back to strategy A, introduced in Chapter 4 and revisited in Chapter 7, we are saying that:

	£000
We have a business which is expected to generate cash, over the next year, amounting to	1,958
At the end of that period, we believe it will be worth	19,583
	21,541
the present value of which, assuming a cost of capital of 15.5%, is	18,650

The cash flow can be analysed on the basis of accounting techniques, eg £2.483 million profit partially offset by a £0.525 million expansion of assets, for incorporation into traditional budgets. Alternatively, it can be analysed on the basis of the purpose of the outlay—volume inducing, anticipative, etc—to assist strategic management.

At this point, we can also note that the projected value, though appearing as a single-point figure, can actually be the result of depressing the midpoint of a range of possible values—the amount of the depression depending on the size of the range and the degree of risk aversion inherent in the business. Thus all of the examples in Chapters 3 to 7 can be revisited on the basis that any figures quoted had already been adjusted for uncertainty as described in this chapter.

FINANCE THROUGH THE LOOKING GLASS

In Chapter 1 we noted how the accounting model has encouraged a 'rear-view mirror' approach to finance. Although cash generation is known hours after the end of a period, it is not reported until weeks or months later, when chosen accounting concepts have been applied to its separation into its profit and expansion components. More disturbingly, it is always reported in anti-chronological order: profits/expansion (ie successive balance sheets)/cash flow.

This inverted view also characterizes the traditional approach to the cost of capital, which, as we have seen, relies on:

☐ last year's balance sheet, to identify capital structure and hence the weightings to the various components of capital. The higher the proportion of borrowings, other things being equal, the lower the weighted average cost of capital;

☐ past share prices, to arrive at an appropriate cost of equity. Common sense would suggest that, if there is a cause and effect relationship, it is the other way around, ie that share prices are an inverse function of the cost of capital (the higher the cost of capital, other things being equal, the lower the share price).

On the other hand, there are some academics who have argued that capital structure is irrelevant. The higher the proportion of borrowings, they say, the greater the risk associated with the equity and therefore the higher its cost, leaving the weighted average the same. This is a useful antidote to the accounting approach but again does not quite ring true.

Table 8.3 throws some light on this issue, in a way which is compatible with the question of uncertainty dealt with above. It shows three ventures, each requiring an investment of £1 million but with different returns (as indicated by midpoints) and perceptions of uncertainty. The greater the uncertainty, the less willing the bankers are to provide finance—especially after their problems in the 1980s—suggesting that capital structure is a function of perceived risk.

On the law of averages, the return on the equity capital which fills the gap is higher. Looking backwards, therefore, it might appear to be the high proportion of equity which is

Table 8.3 An investment of £1 million

Venture Category	A Risk free	B Low risk £000	C High risk
Increase in value over 12 months			
Maximum	155	395	635
Statistically 'expected'	155	195	235
Minimum	155	(5)	(165)
Capital structure			
Borrowings @ 15.5% p.a.	1,000	500	–
Equity	–	500	1,000
Appropriation of return			
Interest	155	78	–
Equity	–	117	235
Total	155	195	235
% p.a. return			
Borrowings	15.5	15.5	N/A
Equity	N/A	23.5	23.5
Overall	15.5	19.5	23.5

causing the higher return/cost of capital, but looking forwards, the cost of capital, like the capital structure, is a function of perceived uncertainty.

The higher the borrowings, other things being equal, the greater the return to equity. This prompts the question of why British companies do not generally have such high borrowings as their Continental competitors. This reflects considerable differences in culture but draws attention to the possibility that bankers' risk/reward ratios may be different (ie a steeper slope) than equity investors'. This topic is vital in a corporate treasury context, but beyond the scope of this book.

We are now in a position to consider the implementation of the approach along the lines which we have been describing.

Going Forward

The more rapidly the world is changing, the less time should be devoted to looking backwards, and the more time should be spent looking forwards. It is not easy, however, to make the transition from a culture which is obsessed with measuring past performance, to one which is concerned with assessing future potential. In this chapter, we highlight some of the attributes of proactive financial management and link them to trends in other functional disciplines.

PROACTIVITY

The principles underlying the practices advocated in this book are not all new. In particular, the idea that value corresponds with cash-generating potential has been around for some time—especially in the minds of people with a grounding in economics. Harnessing it as a basis not only for decision-making but also for monitoring, thereby closing the control loop, is fairly new however. It will not happen without someone championing the cause within organizations—and finance managers are the natural choice to be these champions.

To fulfil such a role, however, will need quite a significant change of emphasis. In the past, finance has often been positioned apart from the rest of the organization, able to supply an independent view because they were not involved in the making of decisions. Their role has been summed up as 'coming along after the battle to count the dead and bayonet the wounded'. This no longer applies, because colleagues need finance to be proactively involved in the making of decisions.

This is most notable at the strategic level, where choices

need to be evaluated. This calls for finance people to be able to think beyond the end of the current financial year, whereas most accounting practices pretend the world ends on 31 December and starts again on 1 January. This means thinking long term and being able to weigh up the relative merits of current profitability and future growth. In many organizations, the obstacles to thinking long term need to be exposed and debated. The English-speaking world seems to have more problems in this area than the rest of the world. Performance measures and rewards based on short-term results are particularly damaging.

Strategy is not the same as planning (indeed, in a rapidly changing environment it is its antithesis) and strategic management is not just about decision-making. The quantitative skills of accountants are vital to the task of strategic monitoring. But you can't wait until a strategy is completed before reviewing it; you need continuous monitoring such as that offered by benchmarking.

Being more strategic means being more generalist—not in the sense of knowing everything about everything but of knowing enough about everything to be able to ask the right questions. The finance function in most businesses is particularly well placed to be able to direct attention not just to problems, as they always have, but towards opportunities. Remember, however, that while problems are usually susceptible to measurement, opportunities require assessment. Transferring the skills of measuring what exists to those of assessing potential is a key task.

FINANCIAL MANAGEMENT

A fundamental thesis underpinning this book, therefore, is that there is a need to separate the forward-looking, proactive financial management role from the backward-looking, passive accounting role. All too often, people carrying out accounting tasks describe themselves as financial controllers or managers, not appreciating that they are totally different. It is impractical to say that the first three weeks of every month are devoted to routine accounting and that financial management must therefore be concentrated in the fourth, as often happens.

To overcome this, it may be necessary to divide the function into two units. Any colleagues seeking the objectively verifiable truth about the past should consult the accounting department; those seeking help with making judgements about an uncertain future should consult the financial management department. The mind-sets required to perform the two jobs are so different that companies which have made the split wonder why they ever thought they should be combined.

The integration of treasury and financial control is very important. The former is becoming such a specialist area that it is easy for it to become detached, but this must be avoided. Two points in this book help to harmonize the interests of the two aspects:

☐ Clarification of the financial objective in terms of maximizing the value of the business—for all practical purposes, the net present value of the projected cash flows discounted at the cost of capital. An objective along these lines needs to permeate an organization if its managers are collectively to manage for the long term.

You will usually find that engineers and production managers are the first to grasp the significance of this objective. For the first time, they are able to put the logic of capital expenditure appraisals into a bigger picture. Don't be surprised if they help progress the concept by asking 'Will you now apply this discipline to marketing and other similar investments?' Choose a product where you are likely to help justify a higher investment in advertising and you will have another ally to spread the word throughout the organization.

☐ Focus on cash flow, which is what you manage, rather than profits and assets which are an 'after the event' analysis. FRS 3 has gone some way towards demystifying the relationship but you need to go further. Position cash flow as the unequivocal difference between distributions and financing—and interpret it later as the difference between profits and expansion. Avoid the rear-view mirror approach which sees depreciation as a source of funds.

THE WORLD IS GOING SOFT

In line with the above, you need to recognize that the single-point precision and accuracy of accounting numbers are simply not applicable to the forecasts used for making decisions and—at the strategic level at least—monitoring their progress. You have to be able to cope with judgements, expressed in toleranced terms, ie with margins of error. It helps if you understand the mathematics of probability, but this is not essential and can be a turn-off for many non-financial managers.

In the same way, the insistence on profits being realized and assets being tangible is not appropriate to financial management. In a rapidly changing environment, competitive advantage is likely to spring from the very investments which are the most difficult to measure and which the accounting model insists are charged against profits. For financial management purposes, think of the benefits expected from the outlay —higher volume, a better price/volume relationship, lower volume responsive costs, etc. The language of accounting is simply not rich enough for financial managers.

One distinguishing feature of financial management is its recognition of interrelationships. Again, the finance function is particularly well placed to be aware of these. Don't let opportunities be missed because they are evaluated too narrowly. Don't, for example, treat mechanization and advertising decisions as individual projects. The lower volume responsive costs arising from the former will increase unit contribution and justify a higher investment in advertising. This will bring higher volume, which enhances the value of mechanization in a virtuous circle.

The same is true of increased manufacturing flexibility and product range. Be warned, however, of the disorientation you will cause when you first ask 'Are you sure you have built sufficient flexibility into the plant, as proposed?' Accountants are expected to ask 'Could you not manage with a smaller investment?'

One of the most important—but one of the most difficult —messages is the need for the financial manager to be a member of the team (as opposed to the scorekeeper or the patrolling policeman). There are faults on both sides with, for example:

☐ Accountants asking 'Are you saying I should believe what my marketing colleague tells me?' The answer is yes, though you may have to tread warily until you have completed the control loop once or twice, ie compared what happens with what was forecast to happen. If this has not been done in the past (eg because what actually happens is compared only with an out-of-date budget) then your management style will be analogous to throwing darts in the dark (no feedback to influence the next throw).

☐ Engineers, for example, saying 'I would not share my judgement with an accountant for fear that it will be taken down and used in evidence against me'. To counteract this calls for monitoring information to be positioned not as a blame-apportionment exercise but as a seeking-after-knowledge exercise. The attitude of the organization to risk and failure may need to be modified. The inherited culture is one which discourages 'scouting' in the unknown and learning from mistakes. Such discouragement might have been appropriate in relatively stable times when the emphasis could be on herding within defined boundaries, but not in today's conditions.

Merely endorsing the principles of strategic financial management will not, of itself, result in the required changes. Costing and budgeting systems will almost certainly need revising. In all cases, the requirement will be to move to a more sharing, teamworking, approach.

BROADER HORIZONS

The focal point of this book has been an individual business in the profit-seeking private sector. Within that, the emphasis has been very much on the making of decisions and the initiation of a monitoring procedure. Before signing off, however, it is perhaps worth stressing that what has been described is only a part of the big strategic financial management picture. It is the place to start, but once you are comfortable with the basic principles you may be motivated to extend its application.

We have said very little, for example, about comparing an updated assessment with the appropriate benchmark. This process gives rise to something like the variance analysis which is seen as part of budgetary control, but all the components are strategic issues. Interpreting these differences in a way which improves decision-making and directs attention to opportunities is an area in which financial managers are currently gaining experience in and which may one day be worthy of a book in its own right.

More immediately, you may wish to extend the application to corporate strategy, ie the level at which businesses are combined so that the whole is worth more than the sum of the parts. In this way, you can assemble the values of the various businesses, plus synergies, to arrive at a value for the group as a whole. If you reach this stage, and you are a quoted company, you might like to compare your value with market capitalization and consider the implications of an alternative financial objective, namely to maximize the company's share price. If this does not correspond with the long-term health of the enterprise, which should have priority?

Corporate strategy embraces acquisitions and divestments —including, within the latter, demerging units where the sum of the parts is worth more than the whole—but those in authority in the centre of organizations (eg parent companies of groups) seem less keen to initiate such studies.

But corporate strategic financial management goes beyond maximizing the net present value of the entity, which is the logical conclusion of what has been covered so far. It also embraces strategic treasury management, which in turn encompasses such topics as capital structure and dividend policy, and a host of new financial instruments useful for hedging interest rate risk (and therefore 'fixing' the cost of capital). We noted in passing in Chapter 2 that the tax system is far from neutral. In today's conditions, most successful companies which choose to grow by retaining profits are distributing more cash (and are therefore worth more) to the tax authorities than they are to their shareholders. This may be inevitable, given the legislation, but there are things which can be done to minimize the adverse effect.

There are also international issues resulting from the globalization of business and the volatility of exchange rates. Most treasurers are qualified to advise, on what is the most appropriate means of hedging a particular foreign exchange risk, but it is the financial controller in the individual business who is in the best position to identify that risk.

An important feature of strategic risk (the most significant form of economic risk) is that you don't have to be dealing in foreign currencies to be exposed to it. A strengthening of sterling, for example, could be so beneficial to an importer as to enable him to steal your business.

Moreover, there are international aspects of strategic treasury management. Where do you raise your capital so as to minimize its cost? Do you hedge the associated risk? Where do you make your profits so as to minimize the proportion of cash flows which are pre-empted for the tax authorities? Some of these problems have only been around since exchange controls were abolished, but you need to manage them within a solid framework of controls.

Finally, the techniques we have been discussing are equally applicable to the public sector and other organizations not classified as profit-seeking (which usually coincides with them getting their income from people who are not customers, but taxpayers and the like). Positioning the cost of capital as a quantification of society's relative preference for cash in different time frames (as opposed to a function of some past share price) means that it can be applied to investments of all kinds—and certainly not restricted to those called 'capital' in private sector accounting.

We have only skimmed over the surface of these extensions, but if the demand is there, they can be the subject of future books in this series. The whole area is a young one and knowledge is being gained at a rapid rate. For this reason, the author would be very pleased to receive comments and criticisms of the coverage in this book and any general observations on the subject matter.

Index